Praise for See Us, Know Us

"A moving testament to what it means to be human. A truthful and deeply affecting book."

—Mary Motley Kalergis, author of *Home of the Brave: Contemporary American Immigrants*

"With more than a billion people globally challenged by disability, we are the biggest tent on earth. But we are a tent with no walls, because anyone can enter the disability community for almost any reason at any time during their lives. Where respect for dignity and compassion is present, there are no limits to what anyone, disabled or not, may achieve."

—Janni Lehrer-Stein, Disability Advocate

"The kind of book that stays with you. Jennifer Chassman Browne creates space for voices that are too often overlooked, and the result is a book that will make readers think differently about disability. I'm grateful this book exists."

—Cory Lee, Accessible Travel Blogger and Content Creator

"A book that does not reduce disabled people to inspiration or tragedy, but instead honors the complexity, dignity, creativity, and humanity of each person featured. This work is important not only for the disability community but for educators, employers, policymakers, allies, and anyone committed to building a more inclusive world.

"The combination of storytelling, poetry, and portraiture creates an emotional connection that stays with the reader long after the final page. This is a beautiful and necessary contribution to the disability narrative."

— Debra Ruh, CEO, Ruh Global IMPACTExecutive Chair, Billion Strong, #WeAreBillionStrong

"People with disabilities have always been resourceful and creative. *See Us, Know Us; Profiles of Disability* ensures that no contribution goes unnoticed. By providing three dimensional accounts of such a diverse group of people with disabilities, Jenn illuminates our triumphs and tribulations to an audience of all abilities. Everyone should hope to foster a universally accessible world where diagnoses have no bearing on the dignity and humanity intrinsic to our very existence."

—Erin Tatum, Journalist, Community Director for Diversability

"I wrote the ADA because disabled Americans deserve rights, not pity. This book delivers that same truth—thirty voices demanding to be seen, known, and heeded. Read this book. Then act."

—Hon. Tony Coelho, Principal author of the Americans with Disabilities Act (ADA)

"*See Us, Know Us* by Jennifer Chassman shines a light on overlooked voices and reminds us that real change is powered by ordinary people doing extraordinary things."

—Theo W. Braddy, Executive Director, National Council on Independent Living

"Stepping into a role as a leader and advocate for the disability community happened organically once my *Breaking Bad* fame introduced what living with cerebral palsy looked like. *See Us, Know Us: Profiles of Disability,* is a welcome example of the ways that we foster change through authentic storytelling that shines a light on those often marginalized. The book gives people with disabilities a moment to feel truly seen in a world that often overlooks and leaves the disability community behind."

—RJ Mitte, Actor and advocate

"*See Us, Know Us* is a glorious collection that, above all, brilliantly illustrates the fact that the disability community is not monolithic but as mixed and varied as humanity itself."

—Ben Mattlin, Author of *Disability Pride* and *Unbound*

"*See Us, Know Us: Profiles of Disability* is a powerful reminder that disability is not a story of limitation, but a story of humanity. This is an important and compassionate work that invites us not simply to look at disability differently, but to see people more completely."

—Alwin Marshall-Squire, Editor-in-Chief, *GTA Weekly*

"*See Us, Know Us: Profiles of Disability* . . . doesn't just provide visibility. It demands the reader to acknowledge that we are here, we are valuable, and we deserve to take up space."

—Sage Nestler, MSW, Founder and CEO of Releasing the Phoenix

"This book is a reminder that talent, leadership, and determination come in many forms. I highly recommend it to anyone who wants a greater understanding of disability, inclusion, and the strength of the human spirit. It is both educational and deeply motivating."

—Debert Cook, CMP, Publisher, *African American Golfer's Digest*

"For too long, society has relegated disabled people to the shadows. Chassman Browne's book brings us into the light by showing the vibrant lives and achievements of dozens of people with a wide variety of disabilities. Their stories project a powerful truth to the world: we are a boon, not a burden."

—Andy Marso, Author of *Worth the Pain: How Meningitis Nearly Killed Me – Then Changed My Life for the Better.*

"*See Us, Know Us: Profiles of Disability* is a very powerful representation of those in the disabled community. I highly recommend this book to anyone who may not understand the complexities that people with disabilities live with as well as those in the community who feel alone and unheard. This book is especially timely in a month [when] we honor Americans with disabilities."

—Alex Garrett, Founder of OneLegUpAlex Media, host of the podcast, "One Leg Up With Alex Garrett."

"Moving, raw, defiant, and dignified—this handsome book opens up a kaleidoscope of human life. Everyone should read it."

—Rhik Samadder

"A humane and eye-opening portrait of disabled people as workers, leaders, creators and citizens in full. *See Us, Know Us* challenges the assumptions and inaccessible systems that obscure human talent—and offers organizational leaders a compelling invitation to look beyond suppositions and appreciate the full range of people's abilities."

—Anne Michaud, Journalist and Author

"*See Us, Know Us*: *Profiles of Disability* delivers a deeply moving and essential look into the lived experiences of the disability community through raw storytelling and striking photography. Jennifer Chassman Browne expertly weaves together intimate profiles and original poetry to challenge our perceptions and foster genuine connection. It is a beautifully crafted, necessary reminder of our shared humanity and the universal desire to be understood."

—Darren Paltrowitz, *Paltrocast.*

"*See Us, Know Us* neither pities nor performs. It simply looks, at last, and amplifies thirty lives too complex and beautiful to reduce."

—Stephanie Bernaba, Journalist and Master's-Level Behavioral Health Clinician

"This book is a gut punch.

"If you think you understand what it takes for disabled people to just show up, read this and be prepared to be wrong."

—Rick Smith, Host of the *Rick Smith Show* and caregiver

"Browne's structure captures the collective and individual personality, dignity, and humanity of her profiled individuals . . . From the start, the collection calls out inaccessible systems—not disabilities—and urges change, prompting readers to '...see the value in me. // Know that // I matter. // Affirm my self-acceptance.' Browne closes with steps for readers to transform into allies, sharing ideas for self-education, active inclusion, confronting ableism, and becoming much-needed advocates.

"Compelling, intimate vignettes of individuals living with disabilities."

—*Publisher's Weekly Booklife,* Editor's Pick

"Photos, poems, and reflections make this collection a powerful statement of hope, achievement, and perspective that should be in the libraries and on the shelves of anyone interested in ability, disability, achievement, and positivity."

—*Midwest Book Review*

"An illuminating collection of photographs and essays. . . . *See Us Know Us* portrays it's subjects in situ, honoring their self-identification."

—*Foreword Clarion Review*

See Us, Know Us

Profiles of Disability

See Us, Know Us

Profiles of Disability

Jennifer Chassman Browne

Portraits by Natalie Brescia

Foreword by Donna Rena Walton, EdD

Torchflame Books
Vista, California

ISBN: 978-1-61153-646-1 (paperback)
ISBN: 978-1-61153-647-8 (ebook)
ISBN: 978-1-61153-227-2 (large print)

Library of Congress Control Number: 2026914672

Title is published by: Torchflame Books, an imprint of Top Reads Publishing, LLC, 1035 E. Vista Way, Suite 205, Vista, CA 92084, USA

Cover design: Jori Hanna
Interior layout design: Teri Rider
Photograph of Puneet Singh Singhal courtesy of Puneet Singhal
Photograph of Charlie Carr courtesy of Charlie Carr
Photograph of Nicole Demos courtesy of Viivi Keinonen

The font, Futura, has been used for the interior layout of this book. It is one of the class of sans serif fonts that are typically more accessible for dyslexic readers and those using screen readers.

Printed in the United States

For Kevin—Always
In love and appreciation for your unending
faith in and encouragement of me.

Contents

Foreword

It was after yet another panel where disability was discussed—but never embodied. No one looked like me. Too often, disability was treated as a footnote, and Black disabled women like me were left out of the narrative entirely. So I stood up—literally and figuratively—and said, "We are not invisible. We are not an afterthought. We are the story."

This book is a representation of that declaration. It is rooted in the truth that disability is not a monolith—it is expansive, nuanced, and deeply human. Disability is not just a diagnosis or a label; it is a lived experience that intersects with race, gender, class, culture, sexual orientation, and spirituality. What binds these pages together is not a single definition, but the shared reality of navigating the world as disabled people and people with disabilities—each story shaped by resilience, creativity, and the refusal to be erased.

Jennifer Chassman Browne is herself a storyteller, advocate, and visionary who lives with a disability. Through her work with New Ground and her own lived experience, she recognized the transformative power of storytelling—not just as art, but as activism. She understands that stories can shift perception, build bridges, and reclaim dignity. In See Us, Know Us: Profiles of Disability, Jenn has crafted a tapestry of voices—stories and poems born from intimate conversations with disabled people and people with disabilities whose lives defy stereotypes and demand attention. These are not tales of tragedy or triumph. They are portraits of truth—raw, joyful, complex, and unapologetic. Each person profiled offers a glimpse into how disability shapes identity, creativity, and community.

Why center disability? Because it is everywhere—and yet still too often erased. Disability intersects with every facet of life. It influences how we move through the world, how we are seen, and how we see ourselves. To ignore disability is to miss the full story of humanity.

This book exists to correct that omission. It is a chorus of disabled voices and voices of people with disabilities speaking in their own rhythm, their own language. It honors the value of stories—not polished for pity or inspiration, but offered as testimony, as legacy, as resistance.

The mission is clear: to amplify disabled lives with dignity, nuance, and joy. To challenge stereotypes and invite deeper understanding. To celebrate the artistry and activism that disability often demands. And to remind readers that disability is not a detour from life—it is life.

Who is this book for?

- For disabled readers and readers with disabilities seeking reflection and affirmation
- For allies ready to listen and learn
- For educators, artists, caregivers, and community builders
- For anyone willing to sit with complexity and beauty

We hope you linger with these voices. That you question what you thought you knew. That you carry these stories into your own circles and conversations. Let these stories illuminate your understanding and deepen your commitment to disability justice. Disability is illumination. And this book is your invitation to see, to feel, and to respond. And most of all, we hope you are moved to act—not just with empathy, but with intention. To advocate for access, to amplify disabled voices, to challenge assumptions and create space. Let these stories stir something in you that leads to transformation. Whether in your classroom, your community, your congregation, your boardroom, or your family, may you become a listener, a witness, and a builder of a more inclusive world. The voices are speaking. The invitation is clear. Will you act?

Welcome to See Us, Know Us: Profiles of Disability. May it move you, challenge you, and stay with you.

With power and purpose,

Donna Rena Walton, EdD
Founder & President, Divas With Disabilities Project

Introduction

When I decided to write this book, I was not sure what I expected the experience of writing would be, but it has been the most unexpected and most amazing experience!

This book consists of thirty profiles, and each includes a portrait, a narrative biography, a poem, and a poem origin story that gives context to the poem. I spent time with each person profiled to get to know them and to make sure that I was representing the wholeness of their personhood and their experience as a person with a disability in the writing that I produced. The narratives and poems are my original work, intended to pay homage and show respect to each person profiled. The narrative biographies provide a snapshot of the complexity and richness of each person's life, and the poems enable the reader to feel what each person faces as they navigate the world as a person with a disability. I hope that all of these elements help the reader to feel informed, moved, and changed.

I'm grateful for the faith, trust, and confidence that the people profiled have placed in me. I am humbled by their willingness to be honest and vulnerable in telling their stories. It's a privilege for me to have had the opportunity to get to know them. I feel like I've made friends across the country and around the world. I also feel like I've found a community that I was just beginning to realize that I needed.

Most of my friends are non-disabled. They navigate the world without having to wonder or worry about whether they'll be able to find a space or an accessible chair in every restaurant, shop, or event that they go to. They can use that brain space and that psychological and emotional capital for other things. It's exhausting and discouraging to have to think about access in all that I do; to think about how I will respond to people who make comments about the way that I walk, and who treat me as an incapable child.

While I have many people who care about me, I carried these experiences alone until I found others who had similar experiences and who helped me to manage the anger and isolation just by knowing what it felt like. Just by sharing a story, an eye roll, or a laugh, they became my community and my support system, and I theirs.

Some of the people whose stories are told here are people I knew before I started this project. Many are people who either applied to be included or to whom I reached out when I began. They are all amazing, unique, and expressive, and, as well, share common characteristics and experiences—both with each other and with so many non-disabled people in the world.

Some of the common experiences that the people being profiled shared with me included a sense that they are a burden to others: their families, partners, and friends. Many of the people being profiled also described their isolation. Sometimes their isolation was a result of not having what they needed (caregivers, wheelchairs, etc.), and sometimes it was a result of their feelings of being judged and excluded when they did venture out into the world. Experiences that had them choosing to stay home, choosing the solitude rather than the exposure. When they did venture out, hoping for connection, often they found alienation.

But venture out we have! It seems that growing a thicker shell is a necessity for people with disabilities who want to engage with the world but face judgment and well meaning but minimizing actions and remarks wherever we go.

We also face barriers that keep us from getting our needs met, from finding work to entering the places and spaces that we'd like to go. These barriers come from the societies in which we live not valuing our participation, not thinking about us as they plan and design their systems and spaces. My hope is that reading about the lives of the people profiled here will move you, will move the needle in your understanding of the lives of those living with disabilities, and will move you to act in making the world more accessible and inclusive for all.

While the experiences of people who are part of the disability community may vary, there are some commonalities I discovered in my conversations that are worth sharing.

We all want to pursue full lives.

We all want to have significant relationships.

We all want to be engaged in the world.

We all want to be seen as people with value and capacity.

We all want to experience joy.

I went into this wanting to tell stories, wanting people with disabilities, who are often invisible, to be heard and feel seen. I hope that this book does just that.

Stories allow us to understand and connect with each other. While we may see differences between ourselves and others, when we hear and tell stories, not only do we come to better comprehend each other's lives, but we also develop empathy. We can be different and still care about each other. When listening, we look for connections, and this enables us to find similarities and shared understandings in spite of differences.

I believe that stories can be transformative, building deep understanding of and compassion for one another. The purpose of telling these stories of people with disabilities is not to have others pity us, not to have others be inspired by us, but rather to recognize the complexities of our lives and to see similarity and difference in the lives that we all live.

I also hope, in reading the stories and the poems that I've written, that people will gain a better understanding of why and how our world, the physical and philosophical, needs to change to be more equitable and inclusive, so as to value the participation and contributions of us all. In this way, this book and these stories enable us to continue to advocate for those living with disabilities. Please join me in reading and telling our stories. See us and know us.

In love and community,

Jenn

A Note on Language and Disability Identity

As I went through the process of talking with the people profiled in this book, I learned a great deal about how people within the disability community choose to see and define themselves. Are we people with disabilities or disabled people?

I came to understand that some within this community see their disability as an integral part of their identity. It is the framework within which they see and experience the world. Their disability is core, it is inextricably a part of who they are, and thus they identify themselves as disabled people.

Conversely, many people with disabilities see their disability as part of their identity, but only a part. These individuals feel that disability is an aspect or element of their identity, but is not the only element, or even the primary element. Thus, they prefer to identify as people with disabilities.

I've been intentional about honoring these preferences for each person profiled, as well as in my writing and choice of book title.

In our conversations, Dr. Walton was thoughtful about this as well: She recognized that in this book, you'll see both "disabled people" and "people with disabilities" used intentionally. Because language around disability is deeply personal, often political, and always evolving. Some people embrace "disabled" as a proud identity rooted in disability justice, while others prefer "person with a disability" to center personhood first.

Our goal is to honor the full spectrum of how people identify. When referring to individuals whose personal language preferences are not publicly known, we've chosen "person with a disability" in order to honor their personhood. When speaking about collective movements, shared experiences, or politicized identities, we use "disabled people" to reflect the language embraced by many within disability activism.

This approach reflects the richness and complexity of our community—not to define it, but to acknowledge it. We invite readers to sit with that complexity, listen deeply, and respect each person's right to name themselves.

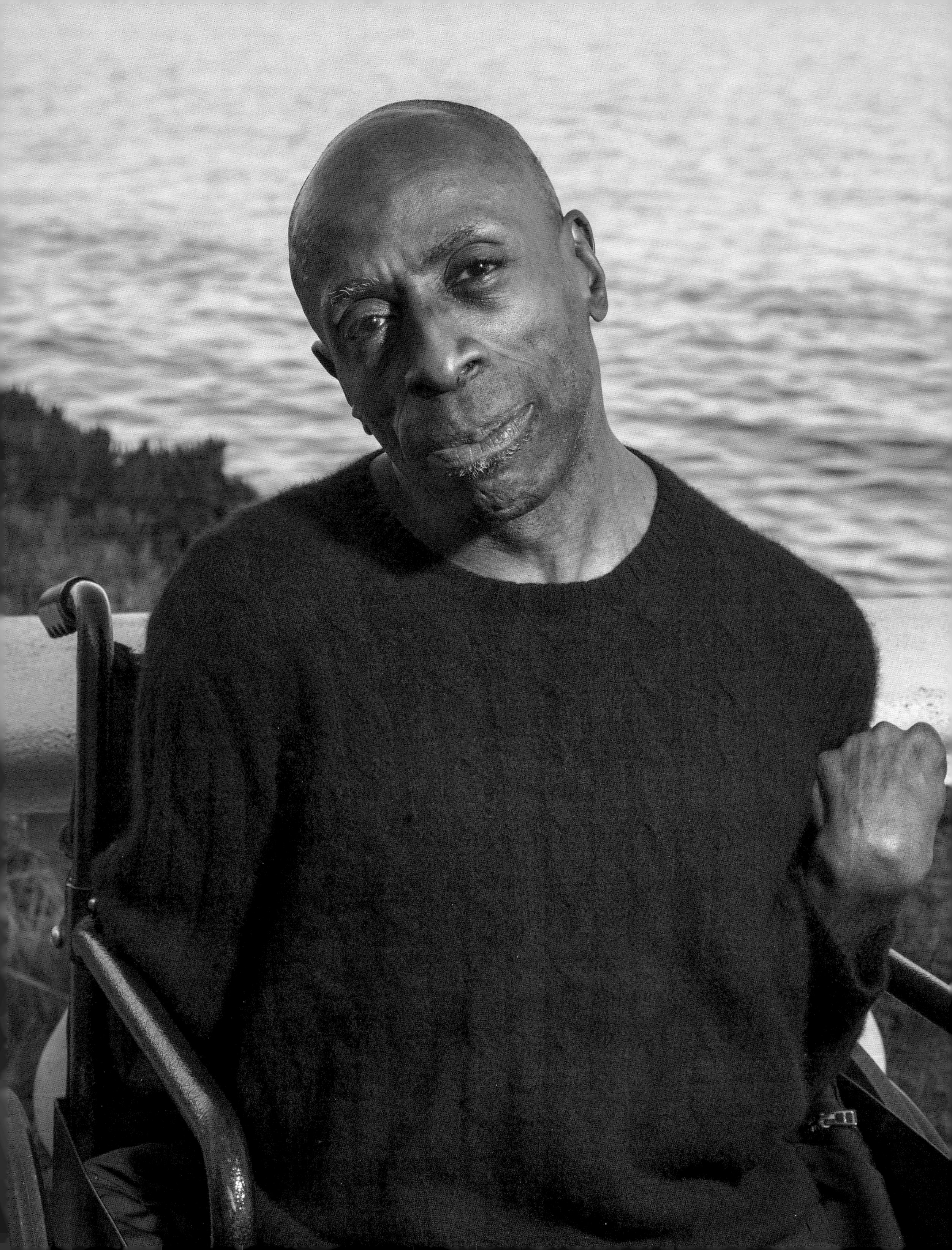

Keith Jones

While Keith had, in his youth, imagined himself becoming a rapper or an aeronautical engineer, when he looks at where his life has taken him, he's appreciative of the opportunities that he's had to make change.

As a child, Keith was bussed to school. He first attended a school for children with disabilities that was like a nursing home and made no attempt to teach him. Later, when he moved from St. Louis to New York, he was again bussed and was often the only Black student and the only student with a disability in his school. However, when he attended Ramapo College, Keith was thrilled to discover an accessible campus and a welcoming community.

Keith says that he "stumbled" into the independent living and disability rights movement, working first in youth development for the city of Boston and then for the Boston Center for Independent Living. In these roles, he started as a tutor and then became a teacher. Later, he worked to change policy related to accessibility in transportation, voting, and buildings, including the Old North Church.

"These are my people trying to come up. Let me go help."

At the VSA (formerly Very Special Arts, now called Access) program at the Kennedy Center, Keith worked as the Boston Art Reach Coordinator, connecting people with disabilities to the arts.

In 2002, Keith launched Soul Touchin' Experiences and has been consulting across the country and the world since then. In his role as a consultant, he has worked to reform systems that have historically kept people with disabilities in institutions so that they now have the opportunity to live at home and have caregiver assistance. In addition, Keith works to change the way that the Health and Human Services Department creates policy for providing Medicare to people with disabilities.

"Advocacy should not be a career path. People should have housing and civil rights without others needing to advocate for this."

Keith's advocacy work has taken him across the country and across the world. He is a founding member of Krip Hop Nation, an Emmy Award winner, a board member, a keynote speaker, and a disability advocacy honoree. He regularly uses art, hip hop, and writing to show the humanity of people with disabilities.

He has worked globally because he recognizes that work is to be done in all cultures where people have managed to find a way to not see disabled people as human. "If this is a movement," he asks, "when will we have moved to a place where we don't have to move anymore?"

Poem Origin Story

Because Keith has been in the public eye since he was young, he is comfortable claiming his identity as a Black man with a disability. His disability is an integral part of his identity. That said, Keith also acknowledges that he doesn't share the totality of himself. There are elements of his life that he doesn't share. As he notes, "Not everybody is entitled to your joy and pain."

Keith also explained that he has experiences in which his disability is used as an excuse not to connect with him or to make others feel validated in giving him (largely unwanted) help and advice. People regularly encourage him to do things differently than he does, in spite of the fact that they have no experience with disability and with disabled people. In interactions with him, others will sometimes "leapfrog" over everything good to get to the disability. When they do so, they are sometimes skeptical of what he does and how he does it.

The challenges that Keith faces are less about the body that he inhabits and more about the inaccessible world that he lives in. He finds many physical spaces hard to navigate and many systems not set up to allow him access and inclusion.

Keith chooses to dream outside of the confines that people have created for him.

Shattered Glass

Just like
Anybody
In any body,
I struggle to
Stay
Whole.

Ableism
Wrapped in a cloak
Of racism.
No pulling
Can separate
These two elements.

You see-
A disabled
Black man
In a chair.

Who can't share
Everything
That he thinks
And feels.

Having
To protect
Myself
To accept
Myself.

You see-
These pieces
I've been
Picking up
Are me.

I wrap them
In
A bag
For safety.
Tie them with
A ribbon.

A million
Little pieces
Of shattered glass
From one.

When nobody's
Looking,
I work
To put them
Back
Together.

Poem Origin Story

As we start to talk about her disabilities, Saran expresses that these conversations sometimes make her uncomfortable. She's found them to be stigmatizing, especially within Asian cultures. That said, she's becoming more and more open to sharing her story.

When she was young, she had a hard time being in social situations, comparing them to freeways. For her, group settings were fraught with traffic: signals that she couldn't read, colors, the meaning of which she couldn't identify, and cars that were sometimes parked and sometimes moving.

This experience could be overwhelming and cause her to shut down or to respond emotionally, becoming frustrated, angry, or crying. She is much better able to engage in these settings now but still finds that sometimes she doesn't understand jokes and doesn't follow social cues.

Saran looks like a "normal kid," so people sometimes doubt her when she discloses her disabilities. This is difficult both because people don't believe her and because when they do believe her, they make assumptions and judgments about her as a result of her disabilities.

Other people don't always see her struggling, so they don't know about the challenges and barriers that she faces. Saran hopes that we can stop making assumptions about each other and start to talk about our challenges. "That's what inclusion is all about; accepting as a community that we are all different."

Signals

Red Green Yellow
Stop
Go
Turn
Right
Pedestrian crossing
Horns honking
Faster
Faster
When what you hear
And what you see
And what you feel
Arrive all at once,
How are you supposed to
Step
Off the curb?

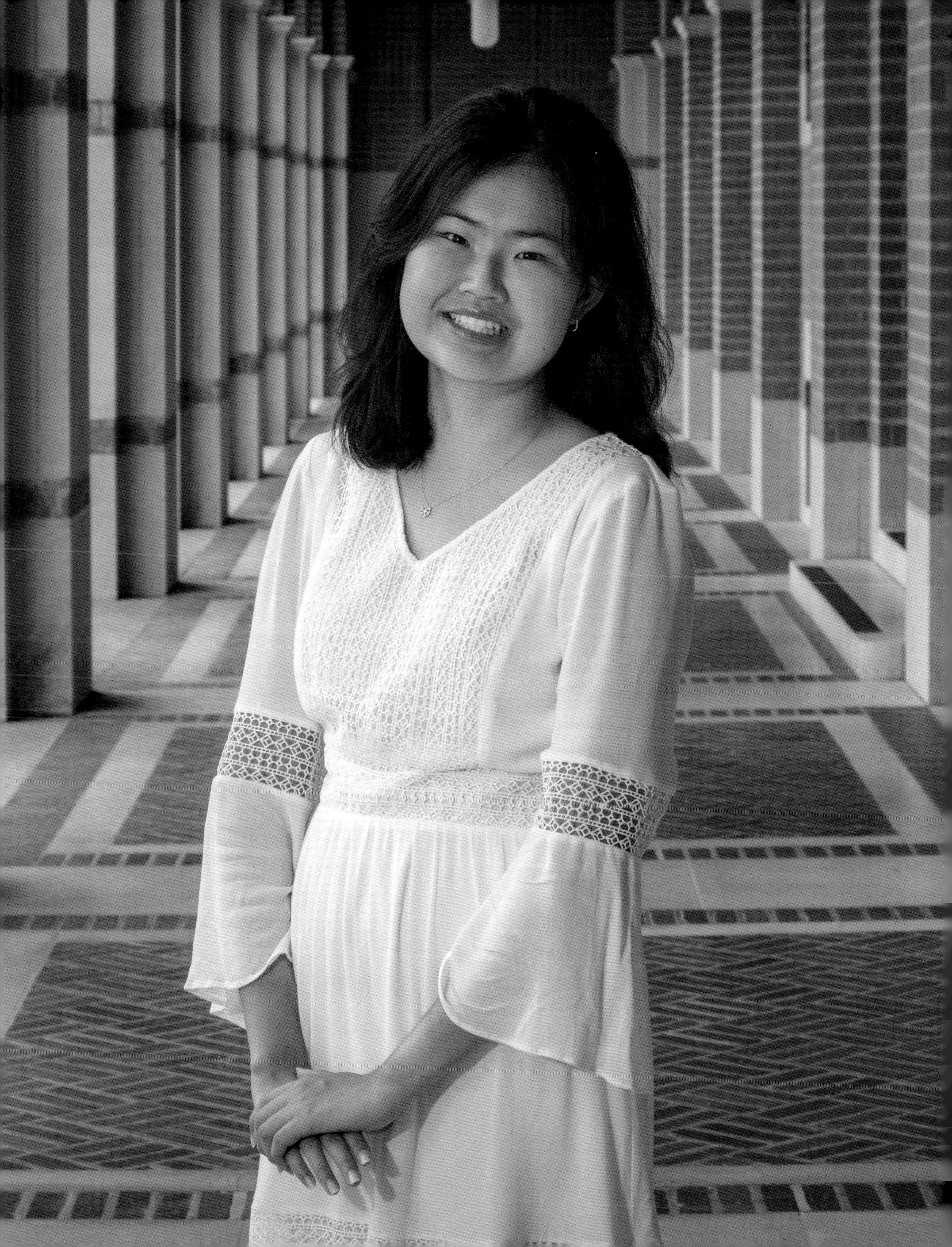

Saran Tugsjargal

Saran is a Mongolian American who grew up in Alameda, California. When she was a child, she was delayed in walking, reading, and writing, and at five years of age, she was diagnosed with ADHD, generalized anxiety, specific learning disabilities, and autism spectrum disorder. It was also at this age that she had an Individualized Education Plan (IEP) created for her. This plan outlined the services that she would receive to support her growth and learning, including speech, occupational, and physical therapy. Saran never felt good about being pulled out of class because it singled her out and resulted in her being made fun of by her classmates.

Saran was raised in a community where, despite the fact that she and other students had disabilities, this was a topic that was never talked about. It was too taboo, too stigmatized, and believed by many in the community to be shameful to have a child with a disability. She sometimes wondered, "Why am I born like this?"

In ninth grade, things shifted for Saran when, after returning to Mongolia to care for her grandmother, her family returned with two of her young cousins. Saran took on responsibility for caring for these five year old twin boys. As she advocated for them, she learned to advocate for herself as well. Ultimately, this led to a desire to advocate for members of the Mongolian community broadly, and specifically, other Mongolian American children with disabilities.

In high school, Saran's commitment to advocacy on behalf of children with disabilities has been a focus for her. She is the first Mongolian American appointed to serve on the California Department of Education Advisory Committee on Special Education. She has also been directly involved in passing several bills in California, including one that changed the terminology for classifying children from emotional disturbance to emotional disability. This will likely be pivotal in enabling children to get care and services that they need.

"There would be a knock at the classroom door ... 'We need Saran for ... testing ... therapy ...'"

"If they don't understand what we've been through, how can they make policies?"

In addition, Saran has worked with the California Department of Education and Disability Rights California to make policies that will enable the juvenile justice system to better serve those with disabilities.

In 2024, Saran was selected as an honoree on the D 30 Disability Impact List. She also attended the Global Disability Summit where she was able to connect people across the globe. It is this ability to make connections that Saran believes will result in making strides to meet the needs of students with disabilities. She is grateful that people with disabilities see her as a resource and come to her to teach her about their disabilities and challenges, giving her the opportunity to learn and to continue to advocate for others.

Saran uses her lived experience to drive change in her community and beyond. She attends Rice University and is studying social policy and political science.

Charlie Carr

In 1968, when he was fourteen years old, Charlie had a spinal cord injury as a result of a diving accident at Revere Beach. He spent months receiving treatment in acute care at Massachusetts General Hospital and Chelsea Naval Hospital, and was then transferred to the Massachusetts Hospital School, a segregated institutional school, where he lived and went to school for the next few years.

After he graduated from high school, Charlie moved to Middlesex County Hospital, a former tuberculosis sanitarium that had been turned into a chronic care facility. Here, he helped to develop a program known as Wellington Hall. Wellington Hall was a separate wing of the hospital where residents with significant physical disabilities went out to college or work. Wellington Hall was a residence modeled after the independent living center that Ed Roberts had started in Berkeley, California.

"I saw what was happening to people like me...I saw the big picture and wanted to make change happen."

At twenty one, Charlie's dream was to live in the community with family and friends instead of in an institution. Charlie and a small group of like minded people lobbied for and co wrote the first Medicaid funded proposal for a Personal Care Assistance (PCA) Program in the country. This ultimately led to the creation of the Massachusetts PCA program funding personal care assistants for people living with disabilities in the community. Charlie was one of the first fifteen people to live independently with the support of this program, which has grown in the last fifty years to over forty thousand people.

Charlie's next step into advocacy came when the Boston Center for Independent Living and the PCA program hired a non disabled director. This spurred Charlie to start his own independent living center, the Northeast Independent Living Program, that provided peer counseling, skills training, and individual and systems advocacy using a peer support model.

Charlie was a co founder for the National Council for Independent Living, which was incorporated in 1982. Charlie became the Vice President, and in this role, he was integral in advocating for laws such as the Fair Housing Act, Air Carriers Access Act, Section 504, the Rehabilitation Act, and the Americans with Disabilities Act.

Charlie has worked to advance legislation that serves people with disabilities on both the state and federal level.

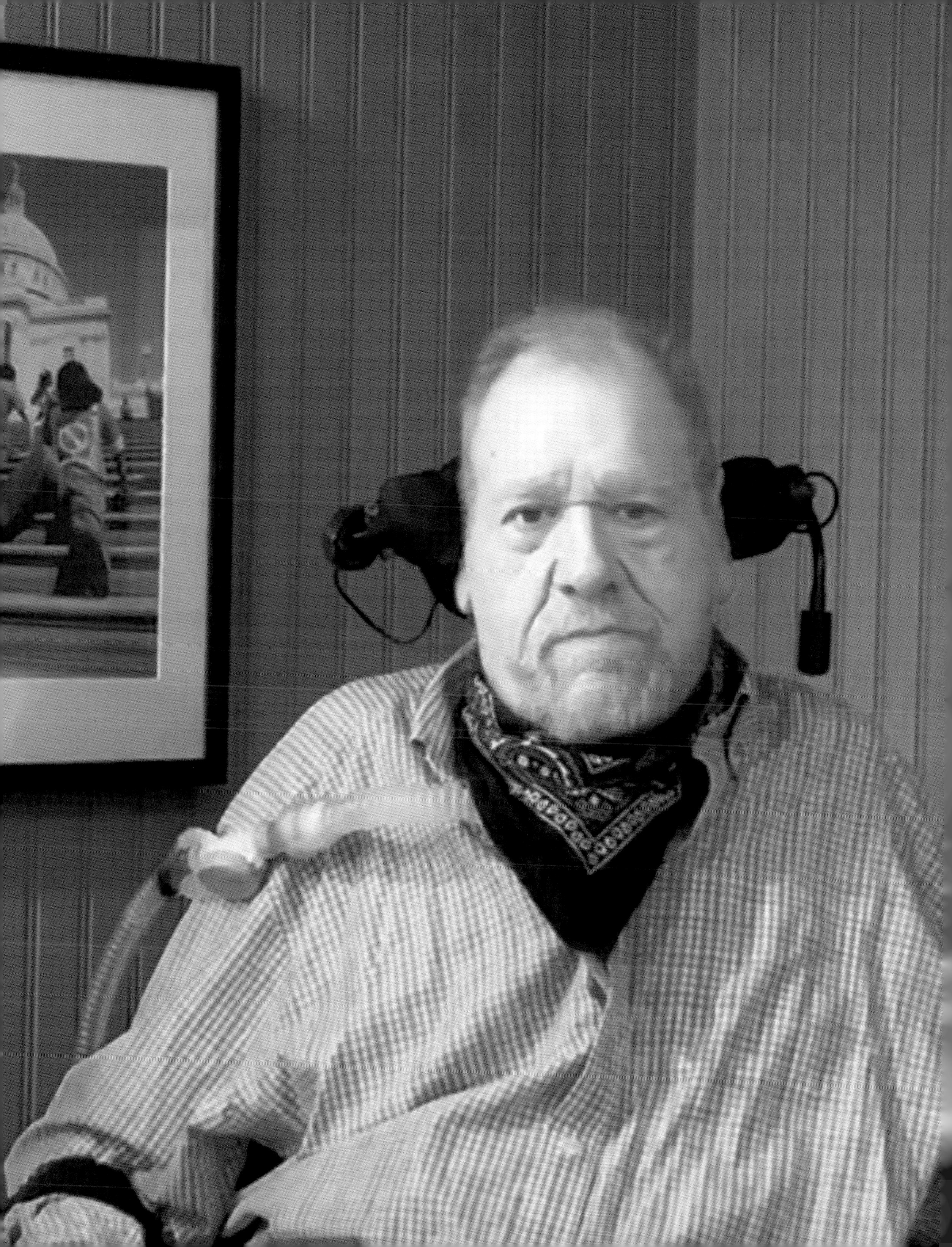

In 2007, Charlie was asked by then Massachusetts Governor Deval Patrick to serve as commissioner of the Massachusetts Rehabilitation Commission. In the next eight years, Charlie transformed the program, transitioning people from nursing homes into independent and community living. Charlie also focused his efforts on working with youth with disabilities, supporting them in developing skills, securing employment, and living independently.

"My work has enabled me to participate in changing the shape of life for people with disabilities"

For the past ten years, Charlie has continued to work in this arena as a lobbyist for the Disability Policy Consortium, as well as a consultant and public speaker.

Soon after his accident, Charlie realized that he wouldn't walk again. Initially, this led to depression and isolation. Charlie was able to channel these feelings into anger and ultimately into a desire to make change for himself and for others living with disabilities. Organizing and leading enabled him to find his sense of purpose. Charlie describes himself as "offering an olive branch with a stick behind my back at the same time," as he was seen as a fighter who was thoughtful and forceful, standing his ground, but also creating allies who became committed to his success and the success of the policies and programs that he developed. He continues to pursue his work improving the lives of people with disabilities.

Poem Origin Story

Charlie pauses when I ask him if he defines himself as a person with a disability. He explains that when he "came up," people with disabilities weren't seen as people. He's a person who happens to be disabled, he continues, agreeing with me when I suggest that his disability is an element of his identity, but not the defining factor.

"People with disabilities," Charlie says, "are people with unique needs." He has made it his life's work to ensure that these needs are met for all who have disabilities. It's important to Charlie that we also know that his wife, Karen Langley, has made it her work to develop programs and services for people with disabilities, as well as to change attitudes that people have towards those with disabilities.

Charlie's advocacy began as self advocacy, as he had been institutionalized after his accident and he couldn't imagine a life without connection to his family, friends, and community. As he made this life for himself, Charlie led the way for and with others.

Most people, Charlie believes, lack an understanding of people with disabilities. They believe that Judy Heumann and Stephen Hawking are the exceptions, when the reality is that many people with disabilities are capable, complex thinkers with an immense capacity to contribute.

Charlie sees himself as a survivalist, rather than a visionary. He's done what he needed to do in order to create the kind of world that he wanted to live in.

Not the Exception

There are names,
Just a few,
That you may know.
Judy Heumann, Stephen Hawking,
Michael J. Fox, Christopher Reeves.
And while they are
Exceptional,
They are not the exception.

Not the only
People with disabilities
Who have the
Intelligence
Capacity
Energy
Skills
To lead.

Most of us do.
Pulling ourselves
Out of isolation
Into a world
Not built for us.
Rebuilding it
As we go.

Solitary survivalists
Who find each other.
And find in each other
The strength,
Motivation,
And community
Necessary
To move forward.
To fight
To be seen
And included.

We are each
Exceptional
But none of us,
An exception.

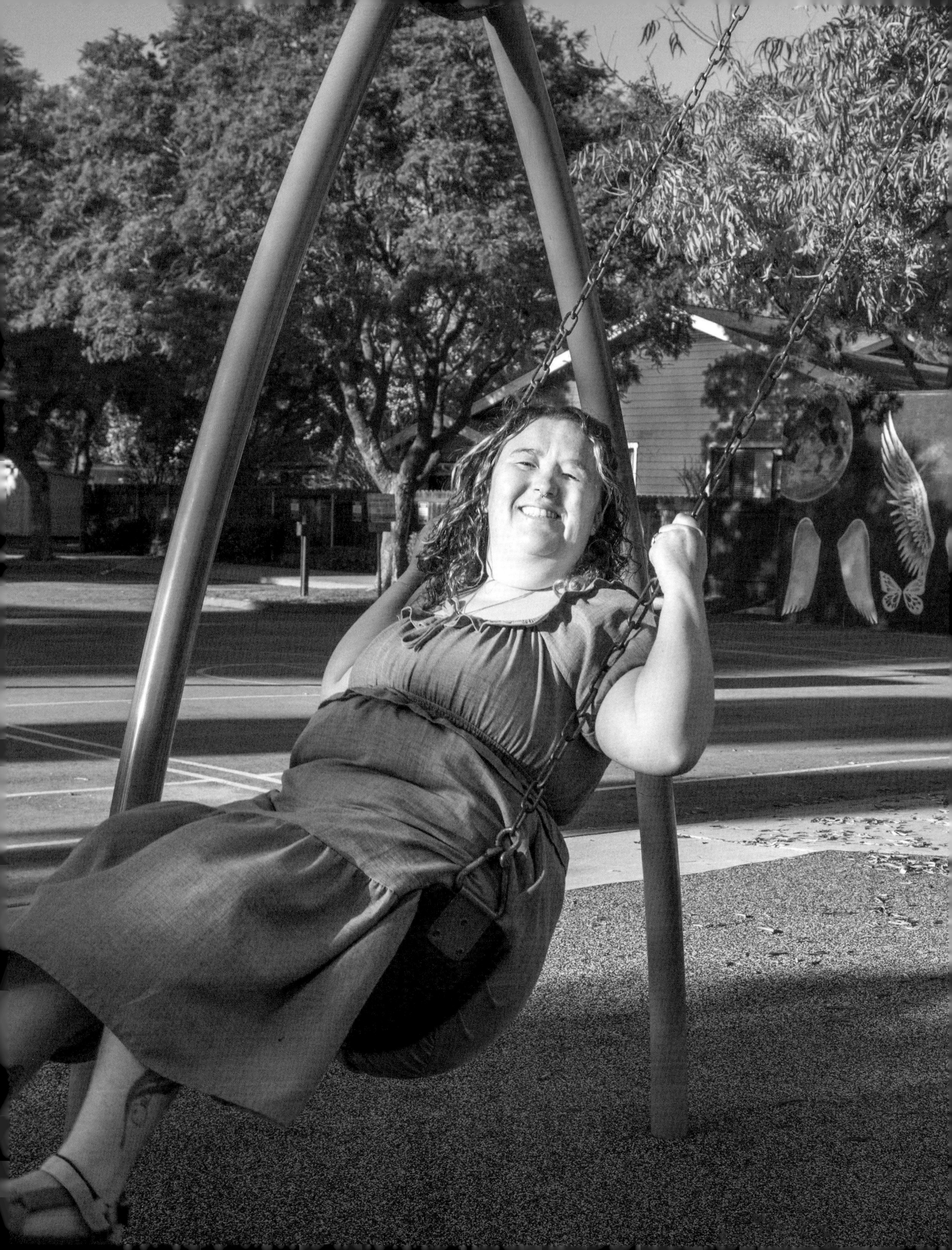

Chelsea Lesner-Buxton

When she was three months old, Chelsea was diagnosed with low vision. It was also determined at this time that she had been born with 60% hearing loss in her left ear. As a young child, she also experienced delays in her speaking and walking, though she was not provided with additional accommodations until the later years of elementary school.

Chelsea continued to have additional progressive decline of her vision and experienced a partial retinal detachment in one eye when she was ten. When she was twenty five years old, Chelsea was assessed as being legally blind. Today, she can see larger objects but struggles to see finite details. She has always loved to read and continues to do so using large print materials.

> *"It's so hard to describe what I see because I don't know what sighted people can see."*

Chelsea is able to hear but finds doing so harder in spaces where there is a lot of background noise. She sometimes wears a pin that says, "please face me when you're talking to me," to help others know that this will help her to hear and respond to them.

As a child, Chelsea sometimes felt left out. She read, heard, and processed information more slowly than the other kids, and found this to be isolating. When she was in school, there weren't any other children with hearing impairments, and there was only one child with a vision impairment, so there were few others with whom she could connect in this way.

Until her senior year of high school, the only accommodations that Chelsea had were large print text materials. In her senior year at Atascadero High School, Chelsea was provided with Orientation and Mobility Training that taught her to navigate streets and intersections as well as to be prepared to ride the bus. This was useful training for her, as she began to take classes at the local community college and traveled there by bus.

It was at about this time in her life that Chelsea began to use a cane. In spite of the fact that she had been reluctant to use a cane, she found it helpful, as it changed the behavior of people around her in a way that made her feel safer. She hadn't wanted to use a cane because her internalized ableism made her worried that others would treat her like a child, believing that she couldn't do things for herself.

After high school, Chelsea earned her associate's degree in early childhood education.

> *"I was so nervous using a cane because I didn't want to be treated any differently."*

Soon after, she went to work for the Independent Living Resource Center as an assistant for the Rapid Response Committee. After that role ended, Chelsea has had several positions as a caregiver for adults with developmental disabilities. She has just completed cosmetology school.

Poem Origin Story

On a recent trip that she took, Chelsea was pleasantly surprised when she encountered a staff member on the ferry who knew exactly how to offer her support. He spoke directly to her, described the route that they would take to get on the boat, asked before he took her arm, and placed himself between her and the edge of the dock. This was a welcome interaction that is all too rare in her life.

Because Chelsea's vision loss was gradual, she hasn't always identified herself as disabled. It wasn't until she had significant loss and she was working at the Independent Living Resource Center, that she slowly began to identify herself this way.

Chelsea has methods that she uses to maintain her independence and to make her home a comfortable place to be. At home, she's particular about where things belong so that she doesn't mix up or misplace her belongings. Out in the world, she mentally maps out the routes that she regularly takes.

At the end of our conversation, Chelsea mentioned that she would like people to know that she is much more than a person with vision loss. When she uses her cane, people are often more patient with her, but they see her simply as a person needing help, without seeing her as the Queer, craft loving wife that she is as well.

Nuances

Everything
In shades
Never sharp;
Light and dark,
Loud and quiet,
Muted colors.
Sometimes relying
On others
To help me
See
The world.
To navigate
It's twists and t
u
r
n
s.
Help
Can be help
Or harm,
Assistance
Or dissonance.
Don't grab the cane,
Don't grab the arm.

Some offer
More patience,
Seeing
This white stick,
Magic
That moves people
Out of my path.
Creating safe space
Wherever it leads.
Though sometimes,
I am left.
Alone.

Vision loss-
A spectrum.
I may not be able to see
you,
But I can see the nuances
That you miss.

Shameka Andrews

When Shameka was born with Spina Bifida, her mother was told that she wouldn't live past five years of age. She's 47 now. The neighborhood that she lived in was difficult because it wasn't accessible for a person using a wheelchair, and as a result, she felt isolated. Shameka was bussed to a school that was an hour away, and even though she made friends here, she wasn't able to see them because they too lived far away.

From an early age, Shameka was a reader and a writer. She kept a journal, and the writing in this journal ultimately led to a children' s book, blogs, and features in other books. She has published two books; a book on self-love and a children's book called, Butterfly on Wheels.

In this book, Shameka tells the story of being isolated and transforming out of a dark place to a place of looking at ourselves in a positive light and celebrating who we are.

Professionally, Shameka has pursued a career in disability advocacy. She has held several roles at Independent Living Centers, helping clients to secure benefits, as well as providing wellness care by offering yoga and meditation classes.

Despite the fact that she didn't feel comfortable as a public speaker, Shameka was encouraged to apply for the Ms. Wheelchair New York Competition. This competition provides women with disabilities with opportunities to advocate for inclusion for people with disabilities. In 2004, Shameka came in third and in 2006, she won the competition. She spent the next year promoting her platform of equal access to education for people with disabilities. Shameka has continued to contribute to this organization and works with others to help them prepare to compete and to promote their specific platform.

As a result of a 2011 Partners in Policymaking program that she participated in, Shameka decided to launch her own company.

Disability Empowered Consulting began with Shameka creating a Disability Empowerment

"My neighborhood wasn't accessible, so I spent a lot of time at home."

> *"I love seeing these young disabled women grow and transform as they find a focus for their advocacy."*

day in Albany. On this day, people could learn about and participate in adaptive sports and other programs for people with disabilities. Since then, her consulting has also grown to include designing and running wellness days, providing accessibility assessments, and providing training sessions on topics including self-advocacy and disability awareness.

Poem Origin Story

Devoted...Intelligent...Successful...Ambitious... Beautiful...Loving...Educated...Determined

This acronym for disabled that Shameka created is immediately what came to mind for her when we started to talk about identifying as a person with a disability. She has never shied away from accepting this term to identify herself, though she feels that it's important to allow others to choose whatever term they prefer. The focus, Shameka believes, should be on the advocacy, not the identifying terms.

Life has been an adventure for Shameka. While most people see her as a positive, grateful person, she's gone through some difficult times of depression during which she struggled to engage with the world. And while she still has hard times, she's actively decided not to let herself dwell in these moments. Shameka has learned that none of her feelings are bad to feel, but she doesn't let the bad ones overtake her; she doesn't let them linger.

Shameka acknowledges that it's hard to deal with daily comments and actions that are examples of people's ignorance of how to interact with people with disabilities. People think it's appropriate to touch her and her chair, ask her invasive questions, and treat her like a child or an object.

While Shameka knows that she can be medically at risk due to her disease, she hasn't let this stop her from living-she loves to be physically active and to travel, and does so in spite of the world not always being a welcoming place.

The Space I Occupy

The sign
On the
Front door
Says,
"All are Welcome."

But I wonder,
How are you welcoming us?
Those who arrive
In wheelchairs,
With crutches and canes?
In darkness
And silence.
What have you done
To welcome us in?

To make sure,
That when we arrive,
We aren't treated
Like a coat rack
Or a footrest.
A statue in a museum,
Or an animal that you can pet.

Some days,
I've had to hide
From this world.
Between pages
That tell other stories-
An escape from my own.

Until
I gather
The strength
To return
To your questions.

To those who need
A disability history lesson
While I'm just trying
To buy a loaf of bread.

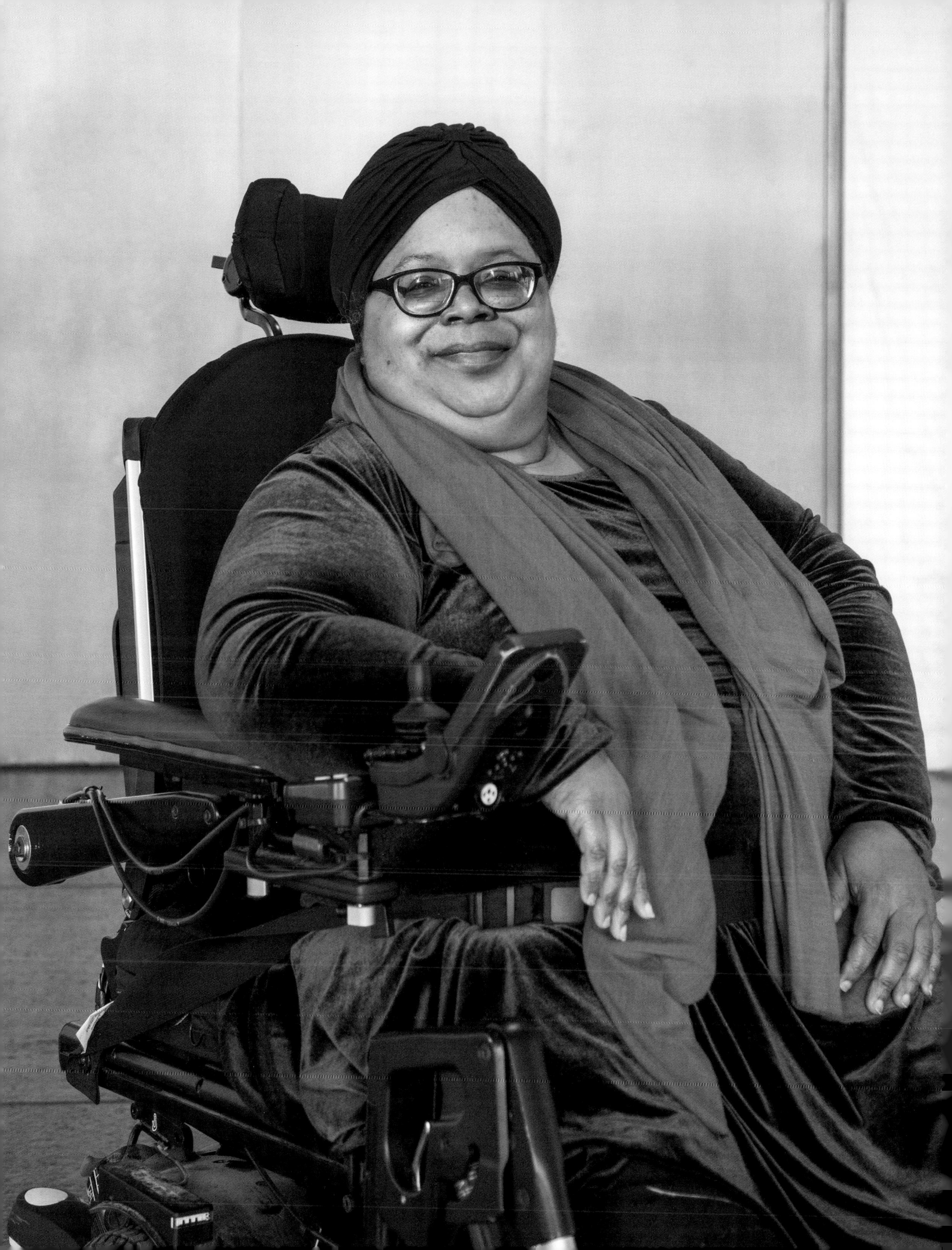

Nico Meyering

Nico was born with congenital central hypoventilation syndrome (CCHS), a rare genetic disease that impacts the body's ability to regulate the nervous system, especially the ability to breathe. His body doesn't hear or feel the signals that other people's bodies do, and as a result, he experiences extremes: extreme hunger, extreme tiredness, and extreme heart rates.

Nico credits his parents for taking fantastic care of his physical and medical needs. They were both assertive advocates for Nico, providing him the foundation that he needed to stretch out into the world outside of the home. His parents started a support group for families of children with CCHS. This group gave Nico a network of other people who understood the challenges in his life. As he has grown, he has taken on mentorship of younger people with CCHS, as well as becoming a resource for other families of children with CCHS.

"I am fortunate to have always had community."

In spite of this community, Nico sometimes feels that he straddles two worlds: the world of the CCHS community and the world at home. Recognizing that, for the rest of his life, his needs would be different from those of his peers, he wondered, "How independent can I be? What does life look like for me?"

When Nico started high school, his mother insisted that he join clubs so that he would have more opportunities for social interaction. This led to Nico being more connected to his peers and gaining social skills. At the same time, more social interactions opened the door to more visibility and more scrutiny and unkind treatment from his peers.

"I gained a sense that life itself is a group project."

After graduating from high school, Nico attended Hartwick College. Here, Nico pushed himself to get involved in activities outside of the classroom. He worked on the newspaper and the yearbook, joined the fly fishing club, and was the VP of the student senate his senior year. These experiences helped him to feel more comfortable in social spaces.

Nico graduated with a history degree and teaching certification. He loved teaching, but not all of the administrative work that came with it. Nico chose to pursue a master's degree in public administration and learned about local

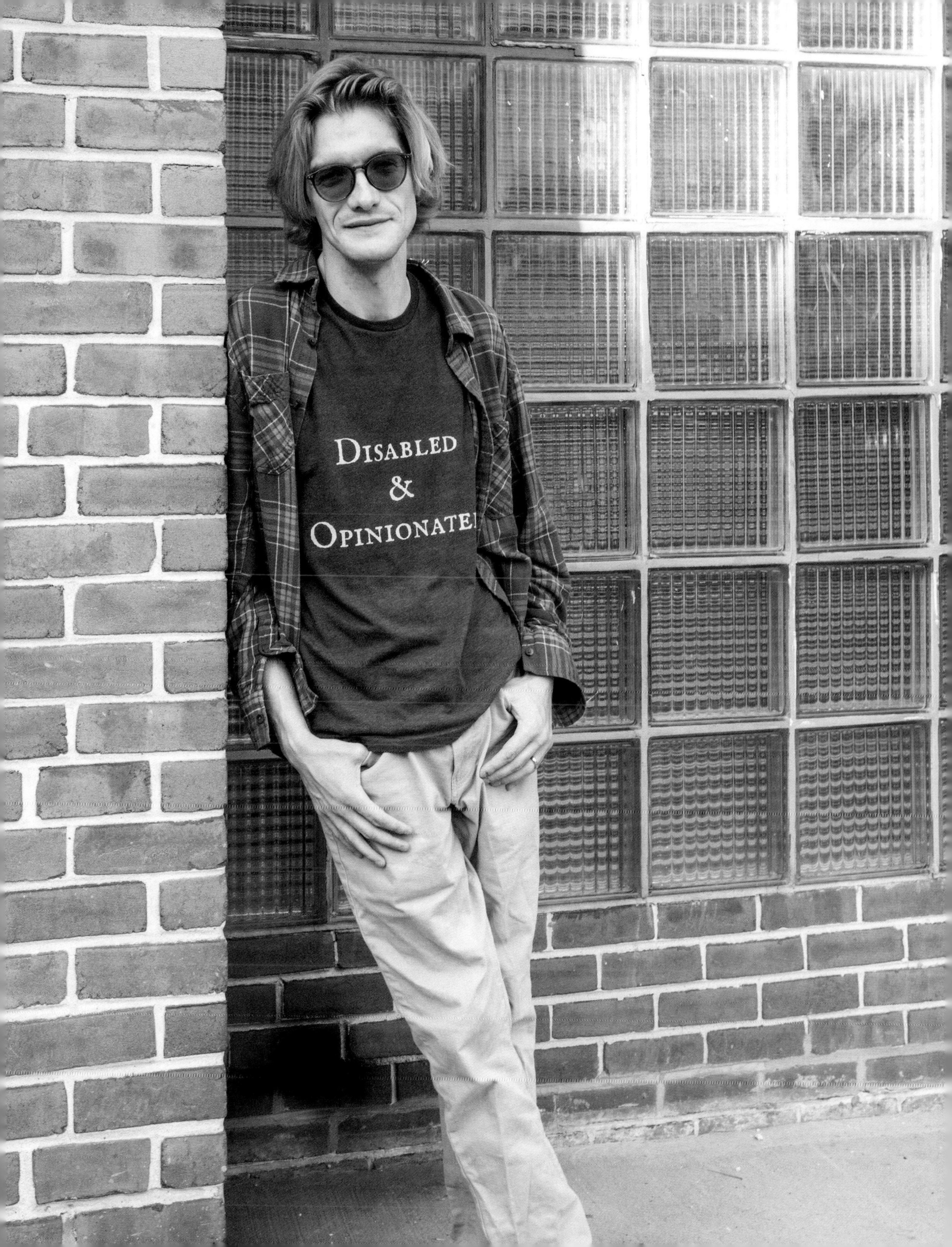
Disabled
&
Opinionated

decision making from local decision makers. He spent two years with AmeriCorps in San Francisco and Texas, doing marketing and outreach for nonprofit organizations.

In 2020, Nico was offered the opportunity to work for the Orphan Disease Center at the University of Pennsylvania. Here, he was responsible for giving grants to organizations that were doing medical research to discover treatments for those with rare medical conditions. He appreciated the opportunity to work on behalf of children and enjoyed getting to meet the children who were benefiting from this research.

While Nico does not still work for the Orphan Disease Center, he stays committed to his work in advocating for those with disabilities in what he calls his "five to nine job." After work hours, Nico chairs the Philadelphia Mayor's Commission on People with Disabilities. He is also the board president for Young Involved Philadelphia, where he works to encourage others with disabilities in becoming board members for other organizations.

Nico is glad to see more people with disabilities leading disability organizations, as he feels strongly that what we really need to see is disabled people leading non-disability focused organizations.

Poem Origin Story

While Nico has lived with his disability for his whole life, he didn't fully identify himself as a disabled person until 2014, when he began to live independently and to manage his own care. For most of his life, Nico's medical needs were most evident during medical crises, and so he hid his condition day to day, as he was able to.

Nico didn't have disabled models to look to; he didn't have experiences of disability inclusion. He associated disability with his own negative experiences and felt ashamed of his condition and his needs.

This changed for Nico when he took on the responsibility of living independently. Here, he found it freeing to be fully his disabled self. Indeed, he feels that it's incumbent upon him to claim his disability and to associate himself with the disability community.

Nico now lives in a large urban area and has a community of disabled people of which he's a part, however he still sometimes feels that he needs to succeed independently. Because his disability is largely non apparent, he can be judged to be "not disabled enough." Often this assessment comes from within the disability community. Nico believes that the more that disabled people speak up, the more the diversity within the community will be evident.

The Helper or the Helped

We seek
To identify,
To categorize,
To make sense of the world.
Simplifying
Identities
That are not simple.

Is he a helper
Or does he need help?

We struggle
To hold
Both concepts
At once-
Embodied in
The same person.

Can one person
Be
A helper
And the helped?

Can a non-disabled person
Reliably hold
This vision;
Reliably
Hold
Disabled perspectives.

Disabled as helped.
Disabled as helper.

If I am a disabled helper,
Am I not
Disabled enough?

If I am a disabled person
Who needs help,
Am I always the needy,
Barred from
Ever being
The helper?

Perhaps disabled interdependence
Is the solution,
As only
We
Understand.

Dr. Sara T. Thompson

Sara imagines her life split into two phases: the pre hearing aid Sara and the hearing aid using Sara. While Sara was born with hearing loss, as a child she lived a life unaware of what she was missing.

One of the first indicators that she was struggling occurred when she was five years old and was given directions by her soccer coach. "The coach would tell me to stay in the game, and I'd be off doing cartwheels and picking flowers." While her parents advocated for her to be able to sit at the front of the classroom and asked the teachers to speak up, not much else was done to address her hearing challenges. Her friends never knew that she was guessing what they were saying, reading their lips and using context clues to fill in the blanks of what she couldn't hear.

> *"All of this plays into how I interact with the world and how the world sees me."*

During her freshman year of high school, her first pair of big and bulky hearing aids made things worse, as they were uncomfortable and made sounds too loud. Despite being hard of hearing, Sara participated in sports and traveled abroad during college. She was a book enthusiast and remained an introvert by burying herself in her studies. Social situations could often become awkward and difficult to navigate, especially with fellow classmates, and she always felt like an outsider. She resisted using hearing aids until her final semester of college when she began an internship.

When Sara worked as a law clerk and her ability to successfully perform professionally hinged on her capacity to hear in the courtroom, she decided to give wearing hearing aids another chance. For the first time, she could hear the leaves rustling in the fall—something that she read about but never experienced. While the hearing aids helped her, the background noises became a new phenomenon to process; she became overwhelmed by the sound of pencils scratching the paper during the LSAT exam.

After returning from her role as a Peace Corps volunteer in West Africa, Sara decided to work in international criminal justice in DC. However, even in this setting, she often chose not to socialize with colleagues. While at the office, coworkers spoke too softly in the quiet atmosphere of the cubicles which deterred the potential exchange of semi confidential conversations; She preferred the setting of small meetings to large meetings and noisy lunch conversations. Her (in)ability to hear depends entirely on the situation.

In her daily life, Sara faces challenges like riding a public transit system that relies on audio

"I hear with my eyes."

messages without visual aids and engaging with others who think she can hear. Because Sara appears able bodied, people doubt her need for accommodations and sometimes misinterpret her hearing challenges for resistance or defiance.

Sara feels conflicted about explaining to others how to best interact with her. She can feel as though she is a problem or burden when asking someone to repeat themselves or explaining how to communicate with her. Throughout her journey, and as a result of being around others with hearing loss, Sara has realized that she is a person with a disability and struggles with the best way to advocate for herself daily.

Poem Origin Story

When she was growing up, Sara thought that people who were disabled were those whose disability could be seen; they were people in wheelchairs. It wasn't until she was in her thirties and using hearing aids that she came to fully acknowledge that she had a disability. "If I have a disability," she then wondered, "what rights, resources, and accommodations does that mean that I have access to?"

Even in claiming her disability, she often feels that she's disabled in some environments, and able in others. She can climb the stairs but can't hear the subway announcements. This has left her sometimes unsure of where she fits, and she struggles with the decision of whether to choose the path of least resistance, or to tackle things head on and choose the path of most resistance. Sharing that she has hearing loss can lead to conversations and interactions that take a toll on her, mentally and emotionally.

There are other costs that Sara incurs as a person with hearing loss. Financially, she has had to invest over $20,000 in hearing aids. It's also been challenging for her to live with other people, as the expectation to talk and hear can be overwhelmingly demanding for her, making her feel on edge. Thus, she incurs the cost of living alone. Because Sara struggles to hear things at work and in the world, she faces the cost of hearing something incorrectly or not "presenting" well enough at work. She may have missed opportunities and connections that hearing people were able to pursue.

Sara believes that generally, people are more familiar with visible, physical disabilities, but often don't know how to respond when she shares about her hearing loss.

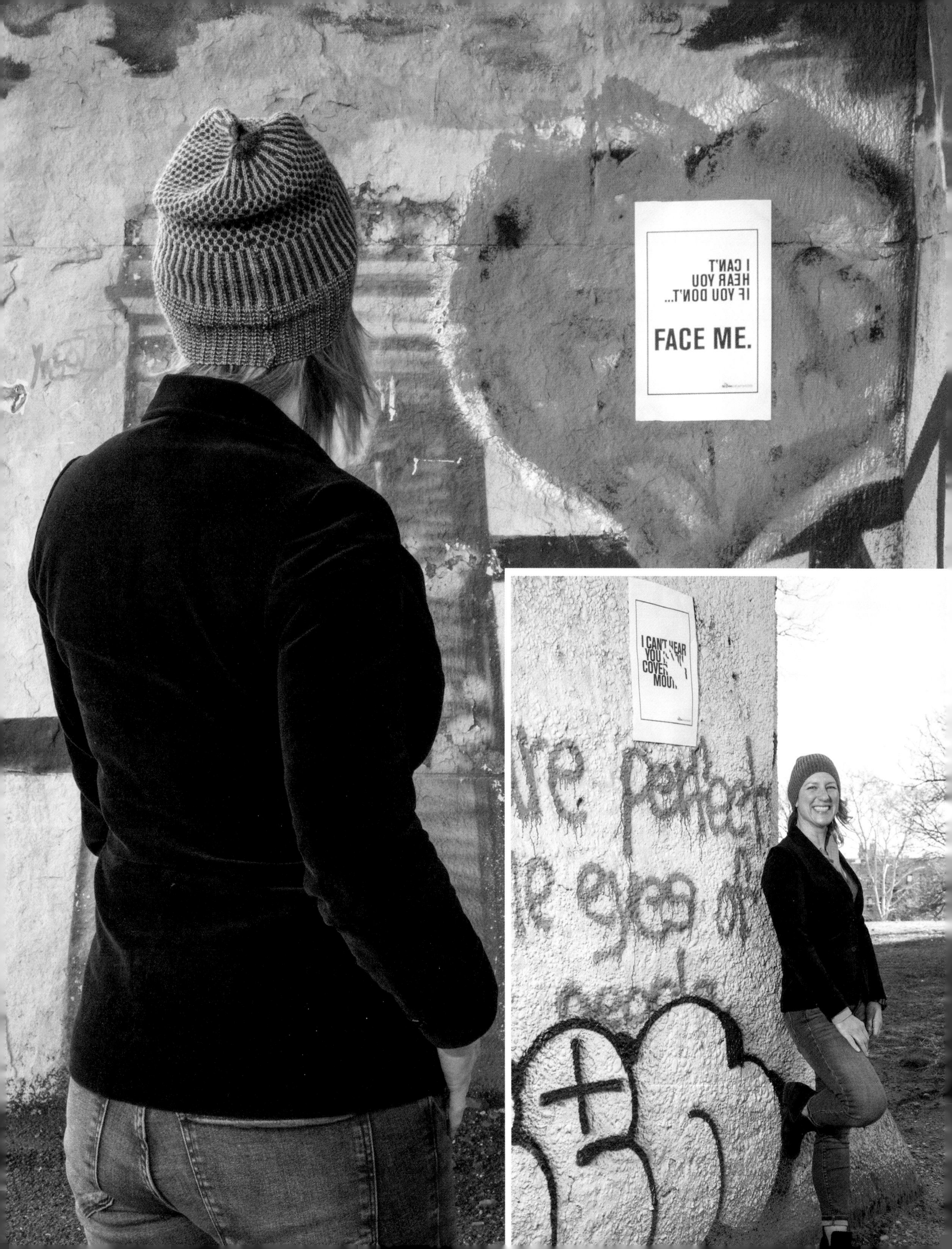
I CAN'T
HEAR YOU
IF YOU DON'T...
FACE ME.
I CAN'T
COVER

Standing Outside

I stand
Outside
Of the circle.

My ears
Reach for your words,
But I am
Unable to hear
What's being said.

Not wanting to
Be a burden
When I
Miss
The punch line.
Or make you
Repeat yourself.

Not wanting to change,
To interrupt,
The rhythm
Of your conversation.

Not wanting
To call out
My need.

If I don't tell you,
You can't see
That I can't hear.

It's hard to
Always
Be concerned
About communicating.
Listening,
Listening,
Listening,
So intently.

It's exhausting
To exert
So much energy-
And to still
Be the odd one out.

I'd like to "chat it up,"
But there have been
So many awkward interactions;
I don't know how to be
Inside the circle.

Isolated,
I hear my own thoughts
And not your words.

Choosing
The path
Of least resistance,
I Take out my hearing aids,
And simply allow myself to
breathe.

Matthew Shapiro

When Matthew was born, he was so small that his father's wedding ring fit on his wrist like a bracelet. Born twelve weeks premature and diagnosed with cerebral palsy, Matthew's disability is a huge part of his identity. Indeed, his disability has led him to pursue his career as a disability consultant.

> *"In order to expose people to disability, we have to be true, authentic, and real."*

It's to his benefit that Matthew is an extrovert, as he has been comfortable in all of the settings that he's found and put himself in. As a child, he had an Individualized Education Program (IEP) to ensure that he had the resources that he needed to be successful in school. In middle school, it dawned on him that he should be a part of the IEP meetings that were about him, and by high school, he was leading these meetings.

Matthew had also taken his brother's advice to heart and still reminds himself to "get involved and stay involved." In high school, he was involved in student government, was the manager for the basketball team, and was first the sports editor for the school newspaper, and later the editor in chief.

When he attended the Youth Leadership Forum, Matthew's focus shifted. He found community with other students who had disabilities, and for the first time he understood that he wanted to be involved in facilitating change. Matthew later worked with the Virginia Department of Education in the I'm Determined project first as a student participant and later as a leader. As part of this program, he was able to shadow lobbyists and meet representatives in the Virginia State Capitol and In Washington, DC.

> *"I'm hoping that in my lifetime, we can go everywhere and do everything."*

Matthew paused his college education to take an opportunity to accept a White House internship with the Office of Public Engagement during the Obama administration. Here, he helped host events with organizations such as the Children's Miracle Network and the Wounded Warrior Project. When the internship was over, Matthew returned to Virginia Commonwealth University and completed his degree in interdisciplinary studies with a focus on sociology, psychology, public policy, and special education.

Since 2014, when he founded 6 Wheels Consulting, Matthew has been working as a consultant, public speaker, and lobbyist to educate and create change for people with disabilities. His impact can be seen in accessible spaces from Dollywood to the Virginia Supreme Court building and in policies including ones that ended subminimum wage payment practices for people with disabilities. Matthew regularly speaks to corporations, to student groups, and at conferences, encouraging them to value inclusivity. He also consults with organizations looking to build accessible spaces. In all of this work, Matthew values inclusion above compliance, wanting to create understanding of and inclusivity for people with disabilities.

Poem Origin Story

Matthew feels like he can't conceive of himself without embracing an identity that includes being a disabled person. That said, he also identifies as son, brother, uncle, friend, and advocate, which he says are elements of his identity that he puts before disabled. He feels strongly that people who are disabled should claim their disability, though he acknowledges that some shy away from doing so, particularly as our society makes being disabled a bad, undesirable thing. "If the messages that disabled people are getting from the current administration are that our existence isn't valued and that we should just die," Matthew said, "how is that supposed to make us feel?"

In our conversation, Matthew also talked about his friends who have shown up and continue to show up for him, supporting him so that he can participate. "They know how to navigate the world with me," he says, going on to explain that they know what he needs with respect to everything from curb cuts to accessible bathrooms. When he's with these friends, he's not the only one thinking about his participation and inclusion.

Indeed, even when these friends are not with him, they think about the world differently as a result of their friendship with Matthew. Changing the way that people look at the world is one of the things that Matthew tries to give to able bodied people through his speaking and advocacy. "We need more able bodied allies," he says, "who insist that people with disabilities be thought about when systems and policies are made, and when infrastructure, including buildings and transportation, is built."

My World

When I roll in,
You know-
I'm different.

I don't fit
Into the pigeon hole
That you've placed me in.

If I can't be in
Inclusive spaces,
I'll make my spaces
Inclusive.
Inviting people in-
I'll be in
Good company.

My best friends?
You see,
They've learned
To ask themselves,
"How would Matthew do this?"
Even when I'm not there,
They see the path I'd take,
See the world the way that
I do.
Can you?

Being alone, though,
Is hard for
This extrovert.

I need
To be helped
To bed, so
Late nights
Don't happen for me.

I have the wheels,
But somebody else
Has to drive the van
Wherever I might
Want to go.

These blurred lines
Compromise
My autonomy.
Though in so many
Other ways,
I'm free.

A son, a brother, an uncle, a friend,
A speaker, a host.
I'm more determined than most,
So don't pity me.

We want the same thing,
You and I.
A life that's not hard,
Not filled
With struggle.
An existence that's valued.

In my advocacy,
I've changed the way
That so many look at the world.
You should change the way
You look at me.

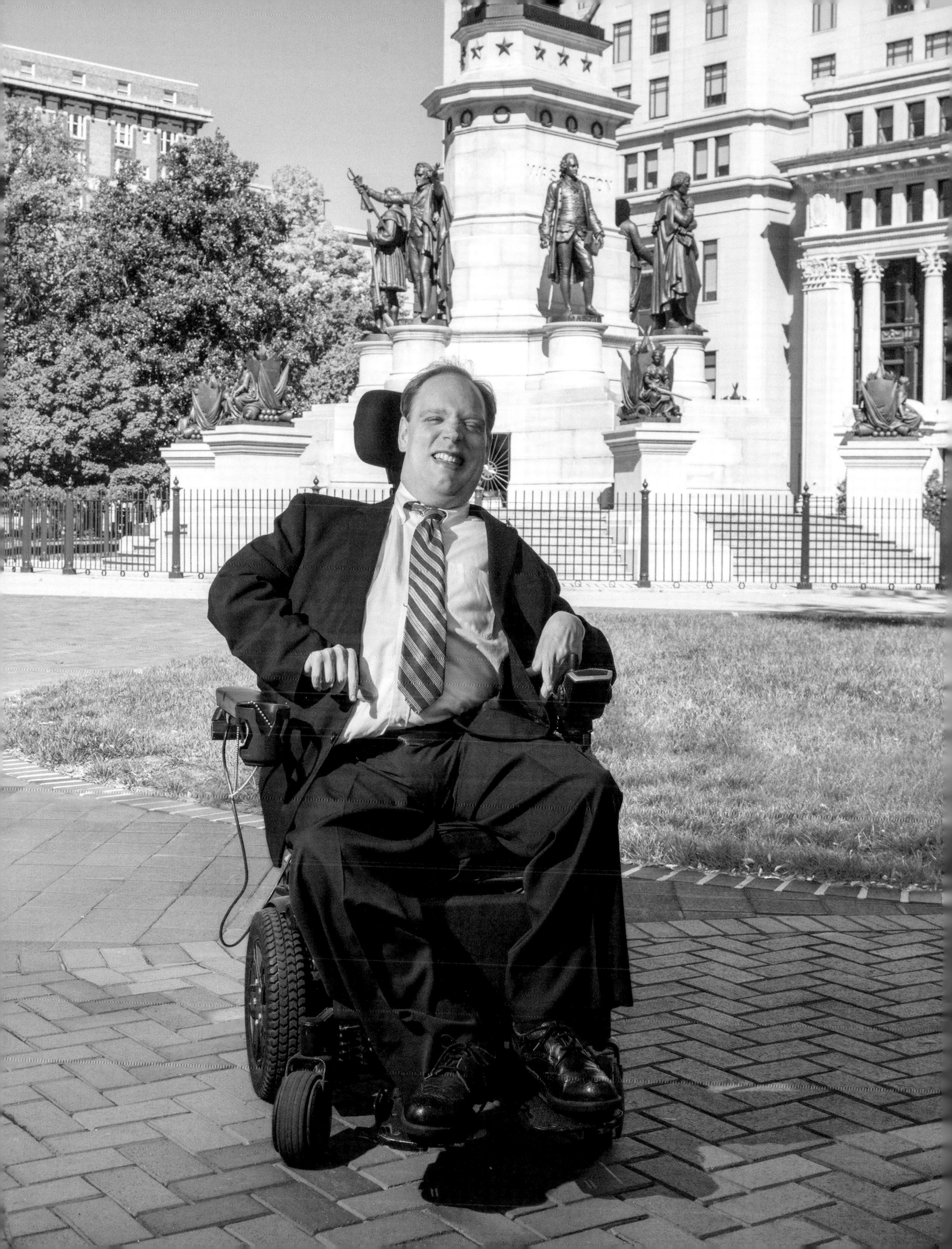

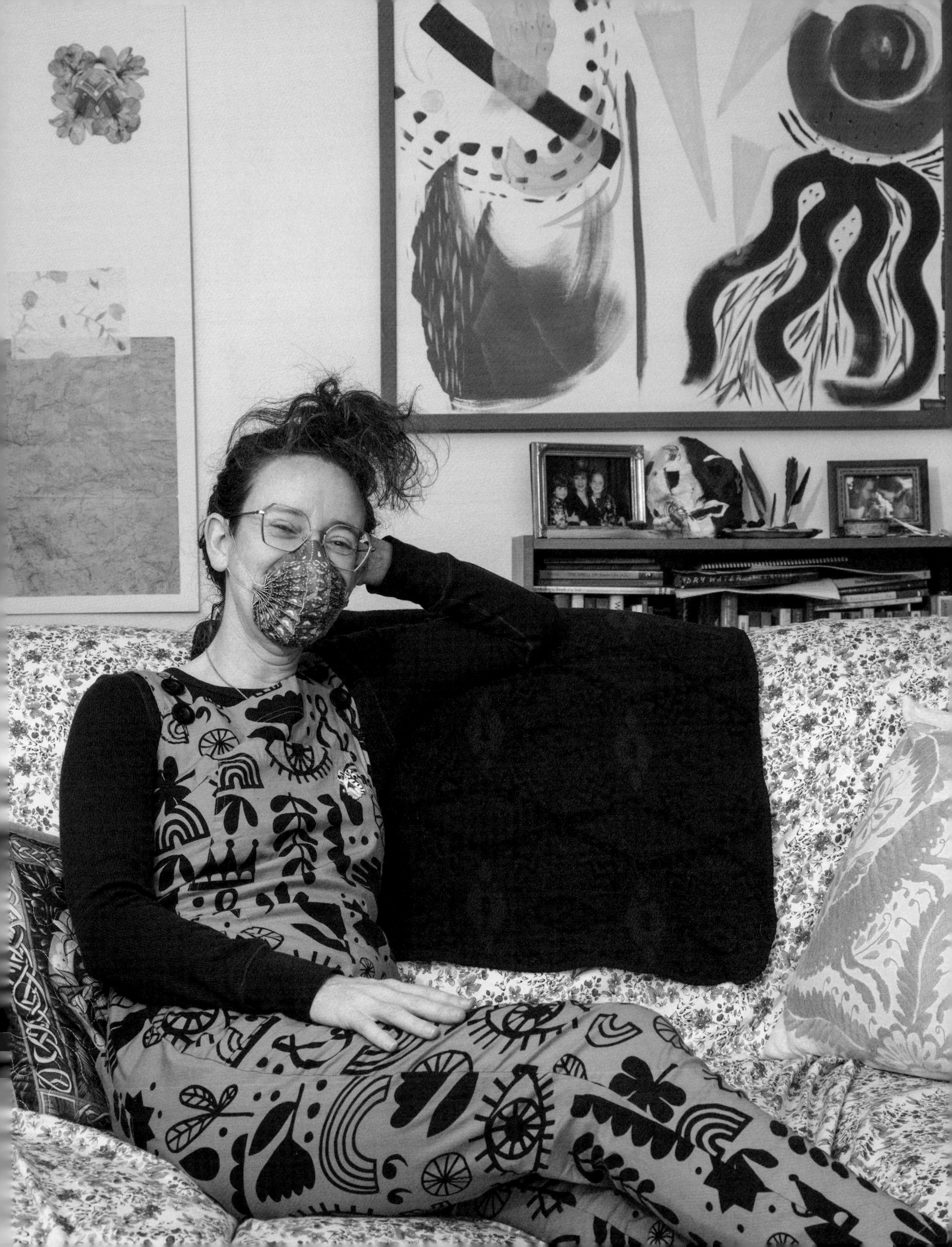
DRY WATER

Kate Levinstein

Kate's experience as a person with a disability didn't begin for them early in their life. As a child, they had an idyllic life. They grew up in Long Beach, California, with their parents and one sibling and were involved with the local synagogue and school.

As a high school student who was studious and deeply engaged in music, playing in the symphonic band and orchestra, Kate was unprepared for the nervous breakdown that they experienced in tenth grade. The last few years of high school were challenging for Kate, and when they began college at the University of Chicago, they felt exhausted. Nonetheless, they enjoyed college, deciding that they were going to, "do this differently," and they studied cultural anthropology and participated in Bhangra dance, taking classes and performing in places like Navy Pier.

After graduation, Kate found it hard to find a job. Because they had taken and enjoyed a first aid class, they made the decision to go to EMT school, and then paramedic school.

During college, Kate had been experiencing stomach pain that they thought was minor. They would just rest when their stomach was hurting and often it would resolve itself. They had become accustomed to enduring and ignoring pain. It was only when Kate had pain that didn't go away and was causing them to be very ill that they ended up in the hospital for three days. In the following two years, Kate was hospitalized five more times.

"Is this what was causing me so much pain all of those times?"

Kate was soon diagnosed with Crohn's disease and had to have intestinal surgery. They continue to take steroids and immunosuppressant medication. Kate struggled to accept their diagnosis and experienced frustration with how Western medicine approached treating autoimmune diseases.

When Kate moved to California, they began learning about acupuncture, integrative and

"Claiming disability means doing community organizing and relating to other people's experiences of being marginalized and oppressed."

holistic medicine, and energy healing. They wanted so badly to believe that they didn't have Crohn's that they bought into everything that they were learning, thinking that they could just work hard enough to control their disease. For a while, while Kate was giving clairvoyant readings and providing energy healings, they stopped taking their medication. Unfortunately, the pain returned and Kate began taking their medications again. Kate decided that they wanted to feel as good as they could, so they began to take care of themself in all ways possible, engaging with Western and Eastern medicine.

It was only in 2020 that Kate began to identify themself as being disabled. For them, this identity is external and political. They feel like they, and other people with disabilities, aren't the problem. "The problem is that the world doesn't slow down for us; it isn't built to include us." Even though Kate works in spaces with members of other marginalized groups, they note that they are often the only one thinking about disability justice. Including people with disabilities is often not the thing that others are thinking about.

Slowing down and encouraging others with disabilities to do so as well feels to Kate like a much more gentle and compassionate way to live.

Poem Origin Story

Kate sometimes has the feeling of being an imposter within the disability community, as they vacillate between identifying their Crohn's disease as an illness and a disability. They acknowledge that they may feel "less disabled" than others within the disability community, as they can take care of themselves in ways that some others in the community cannot. That said, Kate also recognizes many similarities in their life and the lives of others with disabilities.

The fact that Kate is immunocompromised means that they need to mask, sleep and rest often, eat and avoid specific foods, avoid urgency and stress, and broadly, take more care with the tasks of living. They are invested in working on behalf of others to understand that the ways that disability shows up are as diverse as the people with disabilities.

For Kate, their disability is a political identity, as it connects them to other marginalized people who are also engaged in the struggle for identity and inclusion. This relationship with others allows them to be more compassionate and more connected, as well as to dive into what matters.

Kate has to balance this desire for community and connection with their safety and sometimes finds that they feel lonely and isolated as a result of having specific needs that keep them from fully participating. This experience of living on the margins causes others to think that Kate is aloof or not interested in participating. This is far from the truth and Kate feels gratitude for those who have welcomed them in, taught them, and challenged them.

Such a Mystery

I watch
From the edges.
Live in the margins
Between
The hubbub
And my solitary home.

Wanting
So much to be
Known,
And not a mystery.
Wanting to be
Present,
But that which
Prevents me
Has so many layers.

I mask-
My immunocompromised body
Needs this security.
Food can hurt me;
A potluck
Is filled
With risk.

Not choosing to be absent.
I seek connection,
Search for community.
It's not my choice to be a
mystery.

Invite me in,
Ask me what I need
To be known.

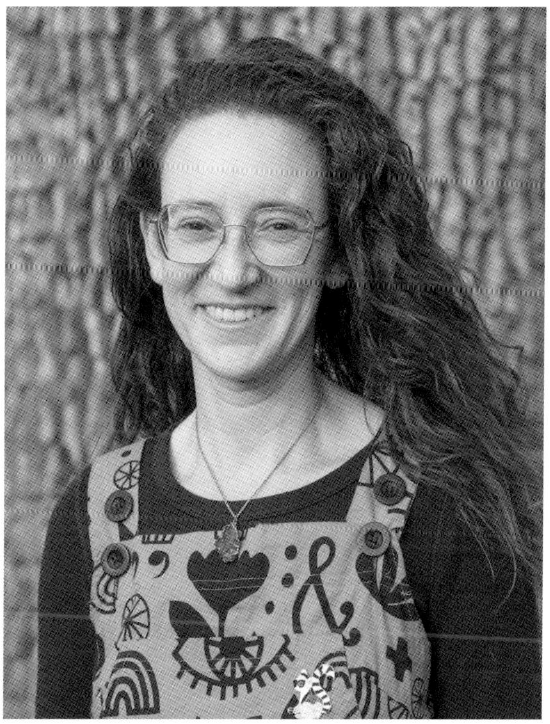

Maxwell Ivey

Raised in a family of carnival owners, Maxwell spent much of his life traveling; setting up and breaking down rides, running children's carnival games, and selling from the food wagon.

From an early age, he knew that he would lose his sight, though for the first six years of his life, he was a typically sighted child who played tag with the other kids in the neighborhood. Maxwell remembers traveling to Disney World and realizing that his eyes were no longer adjusting to changes in light intensity; this was the beginning of his gradual vision loss.

> *"When I do things, I'm doing them as 'the blind guy.' It's sometimes hard to trust in the value of my own abilities and talents."*

Over the next few years, he went from needing a lot of light to read, to requiring glasses, to needing large print books and magnifying glasses, to finally being a braille reader and listening to audio books. All of this change took place from the time that Maxwell was six years old until he was about fourteen. While it was difficult for Maxwell to lose his vision and to no longer be able to read for himself, he adjusted the best he could and even enjoyed being able to contact librarians and get audiobooks to read.

When he was a teenager, Maxwell had the opportunity to go camping with Lighthouse of Houston. This trip ignited in him a desire to be a Boy Scout and he later became the first blind Eagle Scout in that region. This accomplishment led to the opportunity to throw out the first pitch at an Astros game and to be featured in regional newspapers.

After completing his BA in political science at Texas A&M, Corpus Christi, Maxwell worked for a few years and then returned to the family carnival business. He began brokering rides online when his father's passing resulted in the family carnival going out of business. After the business was later sold, he created Midway Marketplace and sold carnival equipment.

People following the midway marketplace website encouraged Maxwell to share more about being a blind entrepreneur. Life changed for Maxwell when he took their advice and started his blind blogger website. In doing this, he chose not to hide, but rather to create content that allowed people to be open about their disabilities. His work as a blogger and podcaster has created opportunities for Maxwell to develop content, speak to and interview others, and to work for accessibility by partnering with a wide variety of organizations. He has written several books, has been involved in creating hundreds of podcasts, and writes for magazines and blogs. He is proud of the fact that his work reviewing accessibility tools will influence how the next version of a product will be made.

Maxwell tried on the title of disability advocate for the first time in our conversation together. Indeed, it was not so long ago that he shifted from calling himself a motivational speaker to an accessibility speaker. Maxwell may be a reluctant advocate, but it is clear that he is committed to using his voice to create more access for people with disabilities.

> *"A limited number of people are coming at this work from the 'positive benefits' side. There's value to hiring people with disabilities and to making your environment accessible."*

Poem Origin Story

Despite the fact that he has some light perception, Maxwell identifies as blind, and not visually impaired. He feels that identifying as blind better acknowledges his experience in the world and makes understanding his disability simpler for others.

Fully claiming his blindness as a disability is a fairly new space for Maxwell to occupy. Earlier in his life, he didn't realize that there was a disability identity to claim. It was only as a result of a talk that he gave at an adaptive technology conference at California State University, Northridge in March of 2025 that he accepted his position as a member of the disability community. That said, despite the fact that he had never planned on being "there" (a member of the disability community,) it feels natural now. He accepts that this is who he is and finds that this acceptance feels natural.

As a result of this self acknowledgement, Maxwell feels more sure about who he is and where he's going. He feels more focused on the accessibility advocacy work that he wants to do.

Maxwell shared that day to day living can still be challenging. He has to depend on flawed systems like medical transit and on imperfect automated scheduling and employment sites. It's also hard for him to cook when he can't see the food, the stove, or the buttons that he's pressing on the microwave. How is he supposed to clean when he can't tell what's dirty? That said, Maxwell is motivated to continue blogging and speaking at conferences and is looking forward to the opportunities that are ahead.

Fishing

When I was
A child,
I loved fishing.

I had to stop
When I could no longer
See
The bobber.

No longer
Know
When a fish
Was on the line
Until it had nibbled away
All of the bait.

Not wanting
To only fish
For bottom feeders,
I gave it up.

Weighted Lines
Are heavy,
And I didn't want
To carry
All of that.

Other people
Kept me
From doing
What I couldn't do.
So I thought
I could
And I always have.

I continue
To cast
My line-
Confident
In my ability
To catch
What will sustain me.

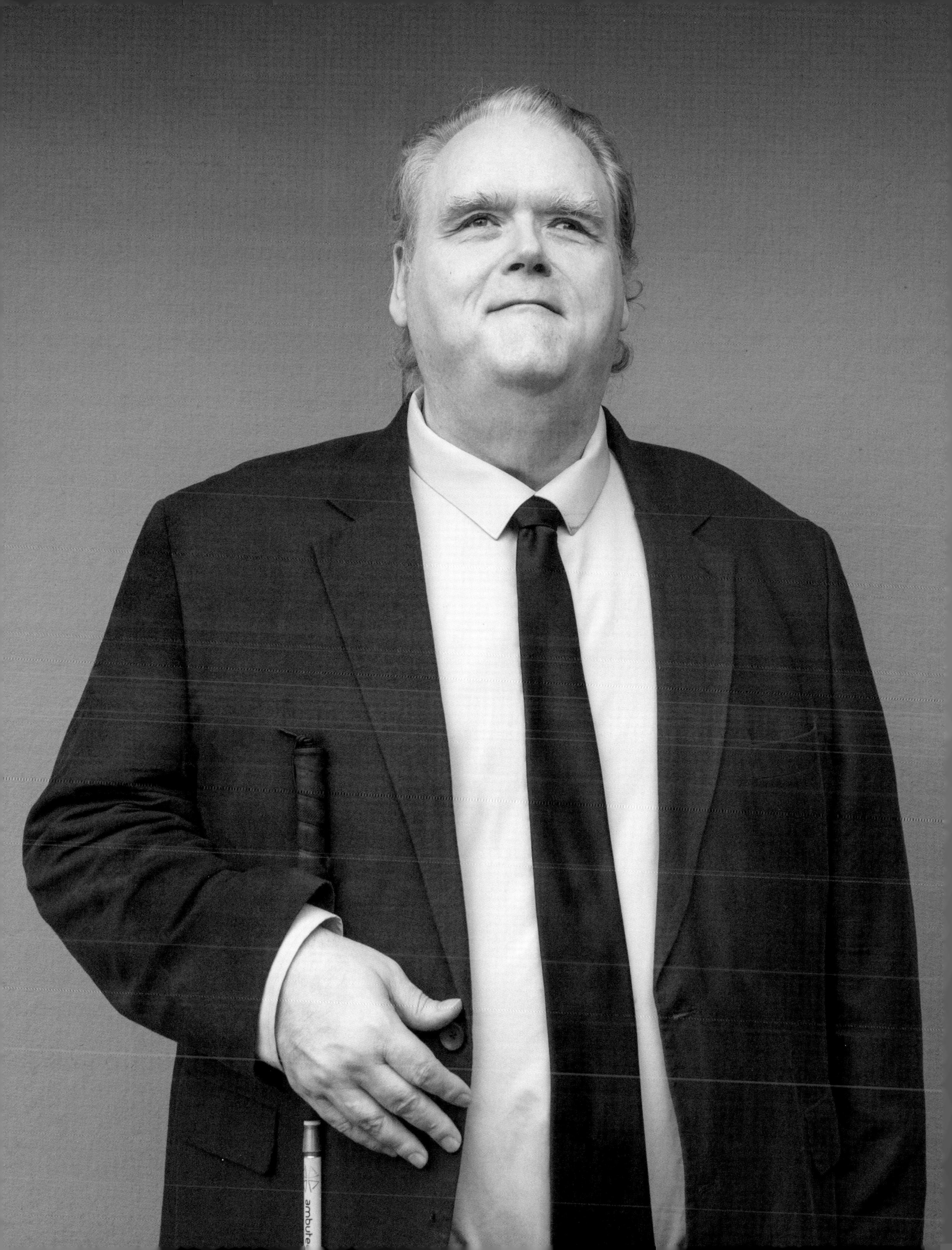

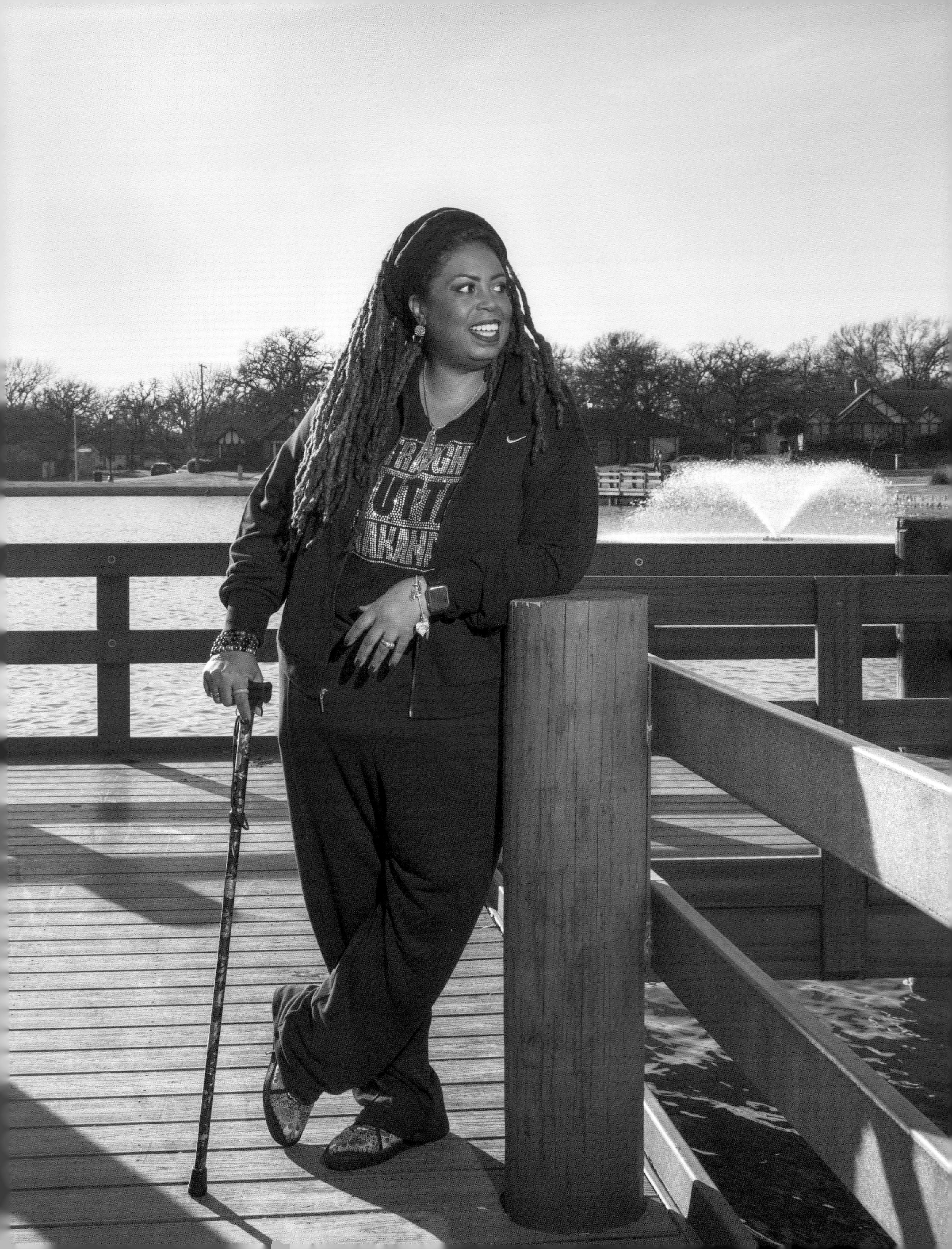

Eve Clark

Eve grew up in Chicago with her parents and her brother. When she was six months old, she came to live with her adoptive family and was formally adopted by this family when she was six years old. Eve has three older siblings: one sister and two brothers. Eve later reunited with her birth mother and learned that she has two sisters and a brother all older than her.

At the age of twenty five, she became ill and was hospitalized. Eve was ultimately diagnosed with multiple sclerosis (MS) and was forced to reimagine her life. At this time, she had been working as an optician, but because of the challenges in her fine motor skills in her hands, she had to step away from this work.

"The doctor delivered my diagnosis in a way that left no room for hope."

Initially, when she was diagnosed, Eve was significantly impacted by her disease, spending most of her time in a wheelchair and experiencing extreme fatigue. She learned that stress, anxiety, and depression greatly impacted her physical condition, and when she was able to manage these, she began to feel better.

In 2003, Eve chose to move to Dallas, Texas, where she started MEB Construction, providing construction services on a national and local basis. She has built everything from clinics to restaurants to daycare centers on military bases. Eve led the company to great success, earning awards for quality and leadership. Her position as the company owner enabled her to have the flexibility to control her own calendar and commitments. This agency enabled Eve to have a healthy work life and to avoid stressors that might cause her MS to flare up.

In 2018, Eve founded Disabled Diva Travels, a travel agency committed to preparing people with disabilities to travel safely and access the accommodations that they need. In founding the travel agency, Eve combined her love of travel with her desire to empower others with disabilities to see the world.

Now retired and a world traveler, Eve has lived in Thailand and Bali and travels for much of each year. In addition to her traveling, Eve serves on several boards. She is committed to working with nonprofits and businesses that are minority owned and champion the needs of youth.

Eve has chosen to focus on staying positive, as she knows that her mindset can significantly impact the intensity of her MS. Sometimes, she struggles with the fact that on her good days, she may not appear disabled, and the world around her may not be able to see the pain that

"My body could be on fire on the inside, even when I'm walking without a cane."

she experiences and may doubt that she has an illness.

The free spirit and positive nature that Eve is guided by have enabled Eve to manage her condition and to support others in doing so as well. She hopes that her choice to pursue adventure and to travel enables others with disabilities to see that physical limitations can be overcome, and to feel confident to pursue travel as well.

Poem Origin Story

For Eve, every day with MS is different. Some days, she is able to walk, and other days, she needs to use a wheelchair. Her mobility and symptoms can change at any moment. This unpredictability, Eve says, is one of the hardest parts of living with her disability. She can quickly go from energetic and vibrant to exhausted and incapacitated.

As a result, Eve has had to become resilient, making choices about how to spend her energy. She's learned that it's okay to say no to invitations and to take time to rest. Her immediate circle of friends understands that each day is different for her, and that she needs to plan with intention. It is also this circle of friends who most fully understand her challenges and needs.

Eve, however, does feel the burden of talking about her disability. She believes that most people don't want to know about it and are specifically confused by her disability because it changes day to day, as she doesn't have the same thing wrong with her each day. Eve also feels this confusion when she is faced with the glares and stares from people who don't understand her disease. Why is she walking one day and using a wheelchair the next? Why is she using an accessible parking space and walking from her car to the store?

Eve's love of travel invigorates her, spurring her on when she's well, and giving her rich memories to recall in her down times. Even on her bad days, she knows that she'll have good days, and she plans adventures for the days to come.

I've Been There

The three pictures
On the wall
At my doctor's office-
All
Places
That I've been.

Seen in person,
Breathed the air,
Touched the stones,
Walked the Great Wall.

The irony;
Being in a place
Where I'm reminded
Of my limitations,
Surrounded by images
Proving
That I can exceed them.

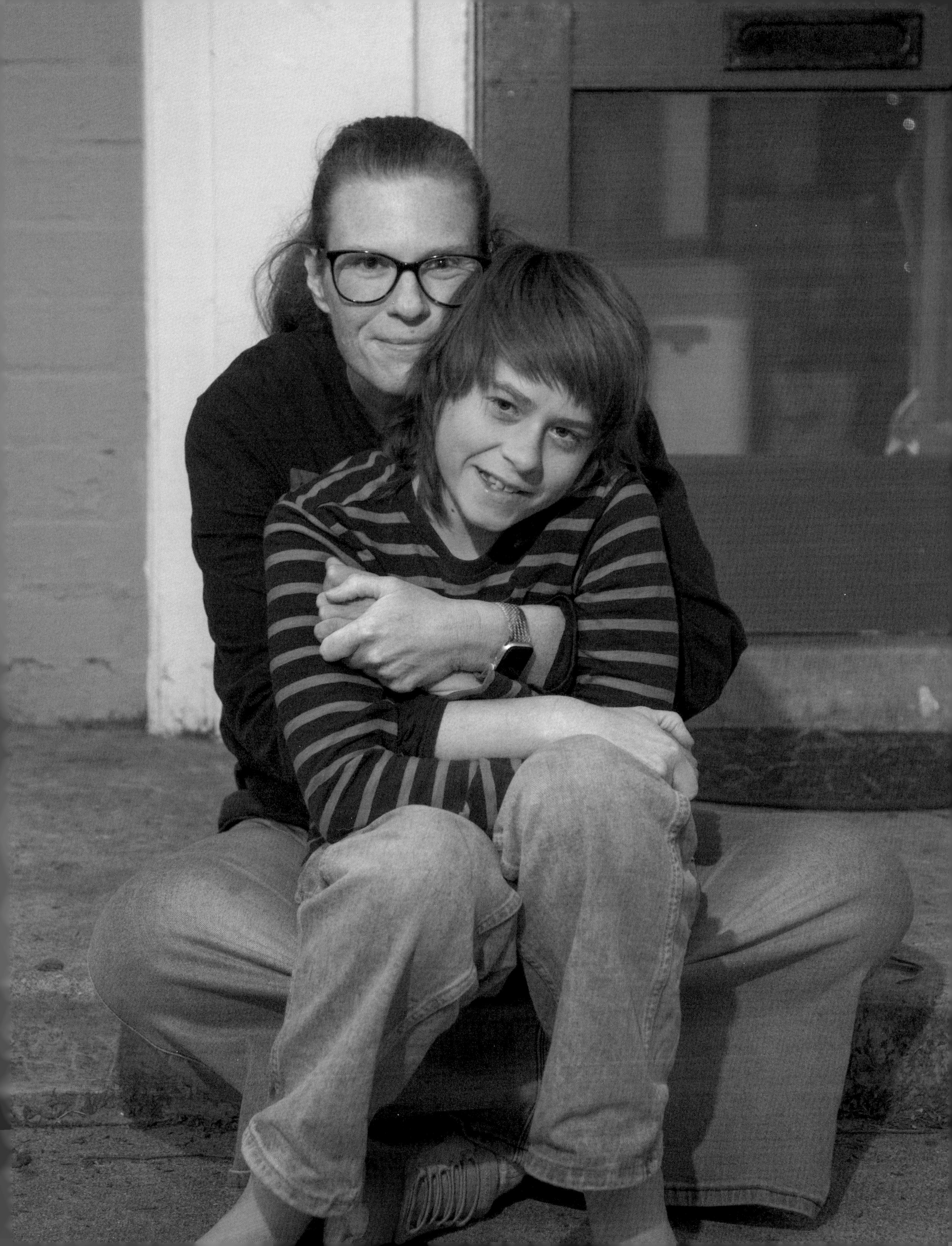

Amanda Murray

While Amanda has been deaf and Autistic since she was born, her deafness wasn't diagnosed until she was a year old and her autism wasn't identified until she was eight years old. She was fitted with a hearing aid, and because there was a stigma associated with raising a child to use American Sign Language, Amanda was taught to speak and to communicate orally. Amanda was able to speak, and because she could speak, often teachers and other people with whom she interacted didn't believe that she was deaf. Teachers believed that she was ignoring them, and as a result of this and her autism, which led to her being developmentally behind her peers, Amanda struggled with communication and with being understood.

School was difficult for Amanda, as disability wasn't really talked about and her teachers discouraged other students from asking her questions. This created isolation for her which also led to bullying. From sixth to eighth grade, she attended a special education school and was in a class for students with autism. While she felt that the academic content was too basic for her, she was glad to be with other students with disabilities and to feel safe. After unsuccessfully trying to attend the local public high school, Amanda was homeschooled until the age of seventeen, when she earned her GED.

Amanda lived with her mother in Romania, where she volunteered at a school for Autistic children. Here, she began to accept herself and to feel pride in what she had accomplished. This gave her the confidence to apply to Gallaudet University, a school for deaf students.

"Suddenly, I wasn't a disabled kid who stuck out like a sore thumb. I was a part of my peer group."

After graduating from Gallaudet with a degree in psychology, Amanda returned home and got her own apartment and a job. It had always been her dream to be a mother, and she signed up with adoption agencies. At first, none of them wanted to place a child with her, but when a child with Prader Willi syndrome needed a home, Amanda enthusiastically agreed to adopt this child. Ash is now ten years old and is a much healthier, happier child who attends the local Waldorf school. Amanda reflects on what she needed as a child when she makes decisions about caring for Ash. She sometimes asks herself, "How did I feel in a similar moment? What do I wish that someone had done for me when I was having a hard time?"

Since graduating from Gallaudet, Amanda has earned an MA in disability studies, and most

"I don't want people to underestimate her as I was underestimated."

recently, she has earned an MFA in film and television production from Loyola Marymount University. Amanda has had the opportunity to participate as an art department researcher for the film Deaf President Now! She is committed to making movies that empower and normalize the disability experience. She is particularly committed to moving the needle for people with disabilities, as she feels like not enough progress has been made and that we're still fighting the same battles that she fought when she was young. She notes that it feels like she's watching it all on repeat from a different viewpoint with her kid.

Poem Origin Story

Amanda prefers to define herself as a disabled person rather than a person with a disability. Her deafness and autism, she says, are not a part of her, they are her.

While she hasn't experienced the world without her deafness, even the peek into the hearing world that she has when she uses hearing aids has made Amanda appreciate the fact that she can remove the hearing aids and live in a quiet, calm space. She can't imagine how hearing people manage the overwhelming experience of hearing everything.

Amanda describes the experience of autism as being a dormant volcano in a world where the sounds are too loud, the lights are too bright, and touch (even accidental touch) is physically painful. When she's overloaded from this stimulation, she's likely to erupt. She makes an intentional effort to ensure that she avoids spaces that bring this on.

"Autistic people," Amanda says, "are often accused of lacking empathy and social graces." But she thinks that it's the other way around. Neurotypical people and the typical world don't make any effort to show empathy to and to practice social graces that would help Autistic people to be comfortable.

I Am Not Something to be Cured

As a child
I lived
Afraid to be
Myself,
To show
Myself,
To accept
Myself, and definitely
Not to be
Proud
Of myself.

Not yet
Seen
As a person,
I was an abnormality,
To be fixed.

Even today
The conversation continues-
We must find a cure
For Autism.
We are taught
To feel sorry
For the poor children
Who
Suffer,
As they say,
From such an affliction.

But I am Autism.
Whole.
Fully and deeply.

Imagine the world
Telling you,
Seeing you
Only
As something
That must be cured.

If I am
Only
Something to be cured,
The world is not
A safe place
For me.

Jennifer Gasner

For much of her youth, Jen just believed that she was clumsy and had sloppy handwriting until, at the age of seventeen, she was diagnosed with Friedreich's ataxia. For much of her childhood, Jen was an active kid—playing volleyball and softball and participating in cheer—in spite of her challenges with her balance. Thus, this diagnosis was a bit of a surprise.

Jen's mother initially only told her the name of the disease, but not much information about it other than that it was part of the Muscular Dystrophy Association. It was 1990 and there was no group dedicated to Friedreich's ataxia because it's so rare. Jen recalls seeing the telethon and having the immediate reaction that she wasn't anything like the people on the screen and didn't relate to them. It was difficult for her to ask herself, "Is that going to be me?" It was only later, when her mother shared a journal with a story about Friedreich's ataxia, that Jen understood the severity of her illness.

> *"Don't let this keep you from doing everything that you had planned on doing—keep going."*

Jen had a rough time in high school and her first year of college, wondering what the purpose of moving forward was if she didn't know what was ahead for her in terms of her health. Things changed a bit for Jen in her third year of college when she went to a convention with some classmates and found navigating the crowds very difficult. For much of the convention, she was pushed in a wheelchair. This experience made her feel safer in crowds and made her more willing to use a walker. This feeling of safety surpassed her nervousness about being seen as a spectacle.

Getting a job after earning her master's degree was a challenge for Jen because she was offered a lot of interviews but was met with "tons of hesitation" when she showed up using a walker. When she was twenty six years old, she fell, and as a result, started to use a power wheelchair.

At this time, she was working as a project coordinator at the Wisconsin Coalition of Independent Living Centers.

Jen made the decision to move to California, and here she has developed strong relationships within the disability community and continued her non-profit work. When she stopped working, Jen wondered what would be ahead for her. She decided to write a book!

My Unexpected Life has been very well received and has led to speaking opportunities and appearances at book festivals, as well as several awards. When Jen found the disability

> *"I wish that I'd had a book like this to read when I was in college. I wouldn't have felt so alone."*

community and learned about disability culture, she better understood the social model of disability that focuses on access and inclusion. This helped her to advocate for herself and others, especially those with Friedreich's ataxia. When she was growing up, she didn't know anyone else with this condition, and now she's able to speak to and for others who share her illness.

Poem Origin Story

Jen begins our conversation by describing the ten year process that she went through before she was comfortable identifying herself as a person with a disability. When she was in college and graduate school, she actively resisted having anything to do with "those people." When she became involved with the disability community, and was working with Independent Living Centers, she started to feel comfortable taking on an identity that she had previously fought.

Even as she was coming to define herself as a person with a disability, she recalls a colleague talking to her about her unwillingness to go to hear Christopher Reeves talk and her resistance to the Jerry Lewis telethon. In both of these cases, the focus was on raising money to find a cure. Jen realized that in these settings, people with disabilities were presented as pitiful, sad, incapable, and needy. This is not how she's ever seen herself or others with disabilities.

As a result of her work with the Friedreich's Ataxia Research Alliance, Jen has learned a lot about the fact that the idea of a "cure" is nuanced. Even within the Friedreich's ataxia community, people experience variety in their severity of symptoms and have different ideas about how much they might need or want a cure.

Most days, Jen doesn't even think about her disability. It's only the treatment of other people that puts her disability at the forefront. She hopes that she can help non disabled people to understand that people with disabilities are capable, worthy, and lovable. People with disabilities can do things, even though they may do them differently. A person's worth is about who they are, not what they can produce.

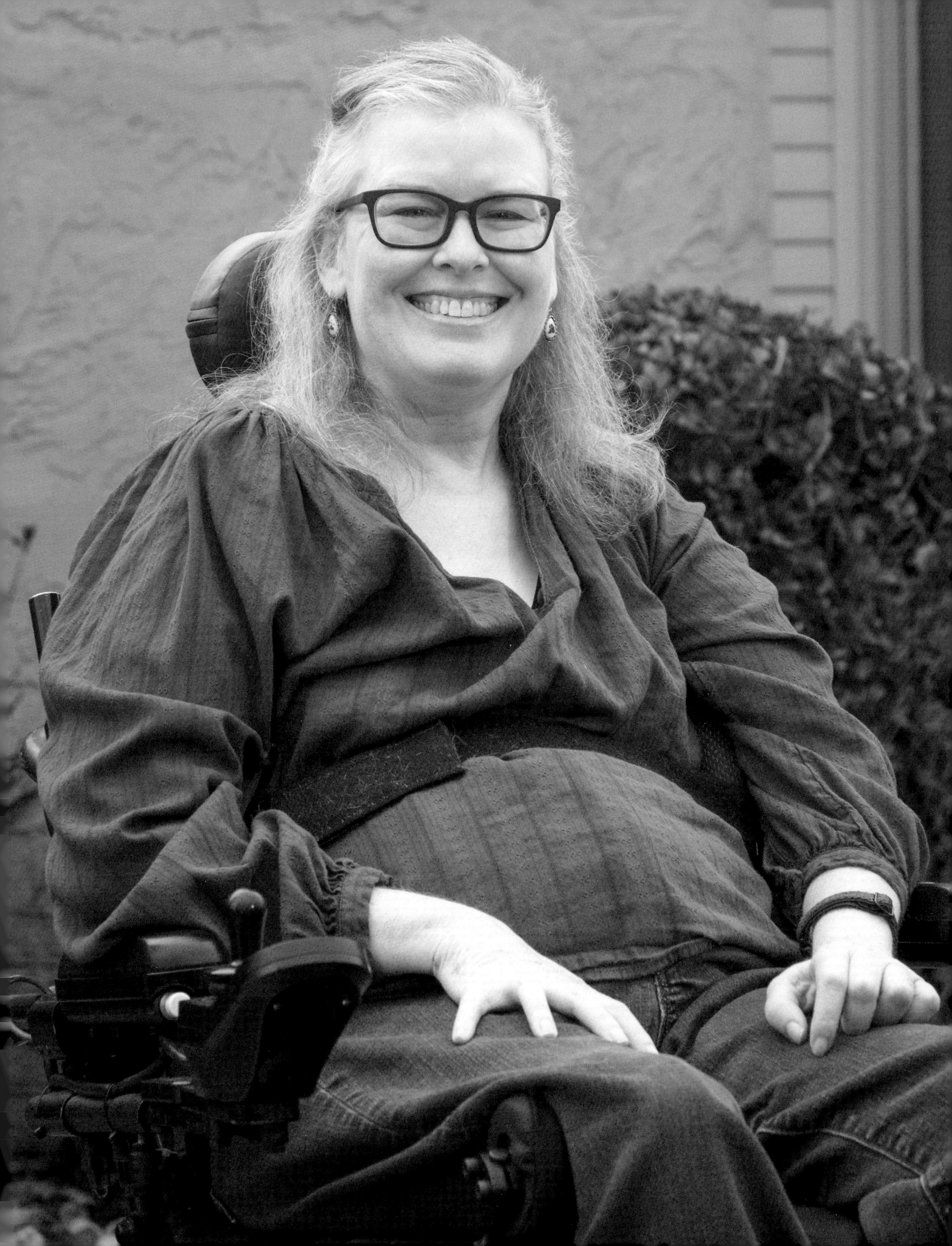

Measuring Our Worth

So often
It seems,
The value of a life
Is measured by what we produce.

People may look at me
And ask;
What kind of a life is that?
What can she contribute?

She can't take care of herself
She's hard to understand
Her vision's not great
Her chair swerves.

In my more vulnerable moments
Of self-criticism,
I'm not fast enough,
Not doing enough.
Have I justified my existence?

And then I remember-
And allow myself grace.

The same grace
That we all need.

You see, I can do a lot.
It's not bad
To need
Help.
We all do,
In one way or another.

I'm intelligent
And capable.
I'm may do things
Differently
Than you,
But I still do
So many things.

And so I remember
And allow myself grace.

The grace
To feel joy,
The grace
To smile.
The grace
To be angry,
Because some things
Are harder
For me
Than they are for you.

Finally,
The grace
To know
That I measure up.

Puneet Singh Singhal

As a child who was born with a stutter, dyslexia, and dyspraxia in the village of Devli, in South Delhi, where life was filled with rapid urbanization, construction, and pollution, there were few resources available to help Puneet find inclusion and acceptance. While he sometimes felt clumsy and had trouble tying his shoelaces, using keys and locks, and riding a bike, he made an effort to hide these challenges. And while he felt vulnerable in being different, Puneet had a strong sense of his own value and never felt inferior.

Puneet was a strong student, in spite of the fact that he was quiet and had hard to read handwriting. He was a good listener and a hard worker, so he did well in school. It was, however, difficult for him to connect with other students who ridiculed and mimicked his speech.

Until he was an adult, Puneet lived with his dyslexia, dyspraxia, and stuttering without a diagnosis. In 2021, when he was diagnosed with these disabilities, he felt validated and relieved. He also discovered resources and a community that provided him with acceptance.

"It was very liberating to acknowledge that this is me."

Puneet used online communities to create connection, writing about his experiences and reading the experiences of others. He was able to read posts written by other disability activists and to realize that he was not alone in his struggle. He'd found a place where people were sharing their authentic selves with the world.

This gave him confidence, and after earning his BA degree in English literature, and a short (and discriminatory) stint working at a bank, Puneet created his own organization. His organization, ssstart, works toward normalizing stuttering and stammering. This organization provides support for people who stutter, including workshops on topics such as listening, acceptance, and techniques for speaking. Members also share resources as well.

"The first step in the lived journey has to be self acceptance."

Filled with the hunger to connect and to do something meaningful, Puneet has dedicated himself to working to ensure that people with disabilities believe that even if they're different, they are not inferior. He is honest and vulnerable in his online posts, and people have responded and been inspired.

Puneet has spoken at the India Neurodiversity Summit and Purple Fest, India's first of its kind inclusive festival that celebrates persons with disabilities and neurodivergent Individuals and is organized by the Indian government. He's committed to empowering youth with disabilities and to educating about the intersection between disability and climate change. Puneet is also the co-founder of Billion Strong, a global disability advocacy group. He was also recently recognized for his social impact by Forbes 30 under 30 Asia and honored with the Commonwealth Innovation award for his contributions to disability inclusion worldwide.

Poem Origin Story

Puneet is clear in his definition of himself as a person with a disability. When I ask him this question, he says that he's in harmony with this characterization of himself. His disability has always been visible, so in totally accepting himself, he has come to fully accept his disability.

When he was younger, he struggled with this identity, as he thought that a confident person and a leader couldn't also be a person with a disability. He is glad that in India, and much of the rest of the world, people who are neurodiverse are also acknowledged as part of the disability community.

Because Puneet is willing to be self conscious, vulnerable, and to share his struggles, he is able to be a leader within the disability community and an advocate for disability rights more broadly. He explains, "I have a goal that's bigger than my personal struggles.... We are valid in our leadership as well."

Puneet is frustrated to still see people with disabilities at the back of the queue. While he sees progress in the visibility and acceptance of people with disabilities, he still feels that there is more to be done. We all need to create a world where we talk about disability and where non disabled people engage with people with disabilities, creating systems that build inclusion.

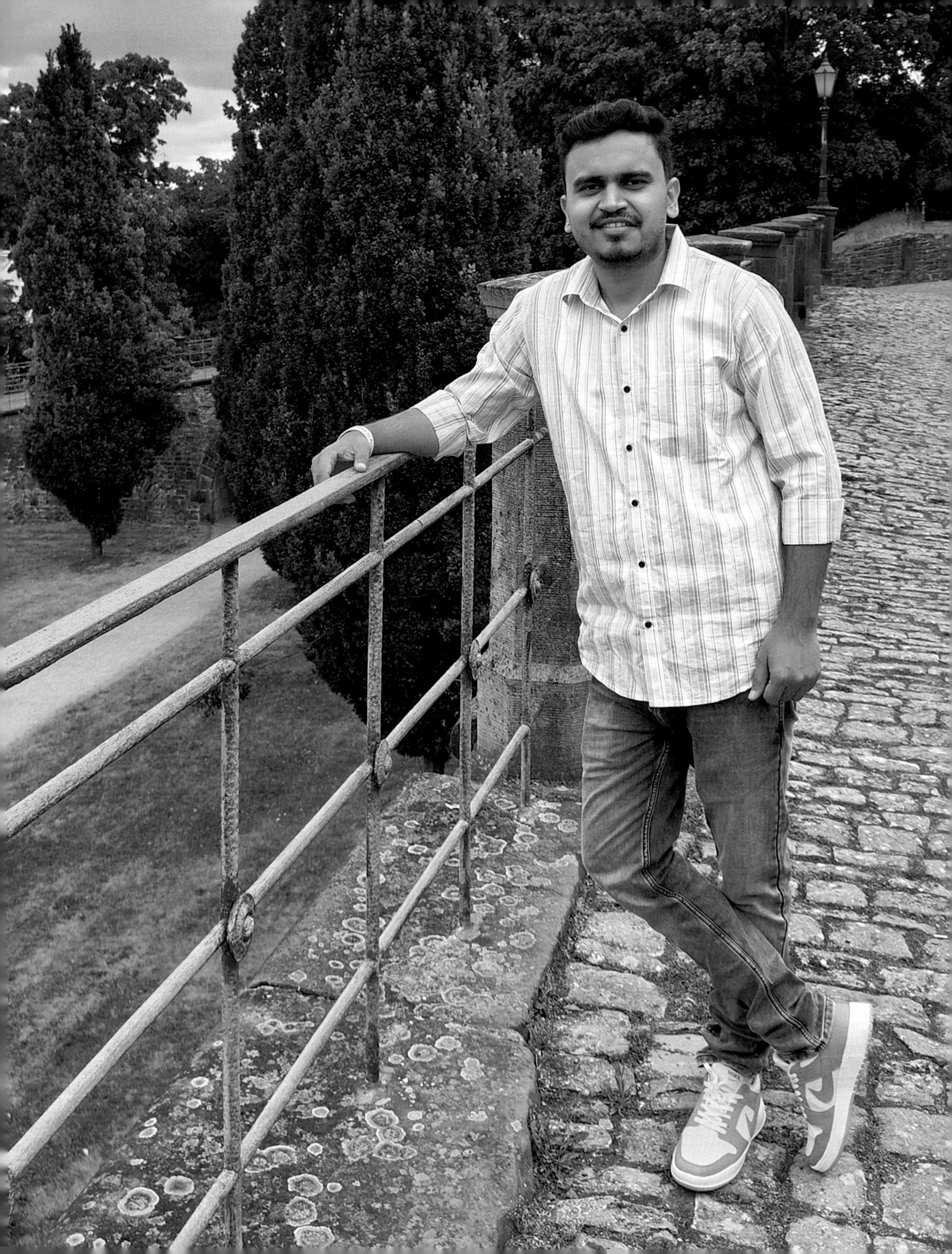

Becoming Visible

I was bullied
For
Saying
Saying
Saying
Things more than once.

But it seems
You haven't
Yet
Understood
My message.

And so
I must repeat myself.

I used to hide
My hands
As they struggled
With discrete tasks;
Writing, cutting, tying my shoes.

But this is me
Messy and unpolished
Raw and real.

This self-awareness, sexy...
It's attractive
To see-
People
Being
Who they are.

When we know ourselves
We can be ourselves-
Natural, naked
And confident at the same time.

What divides us
Is so small,
Unimportant.

We are not just
A wheelchair symbol.
The images that designate us
Also growing
More diverse
Each day.

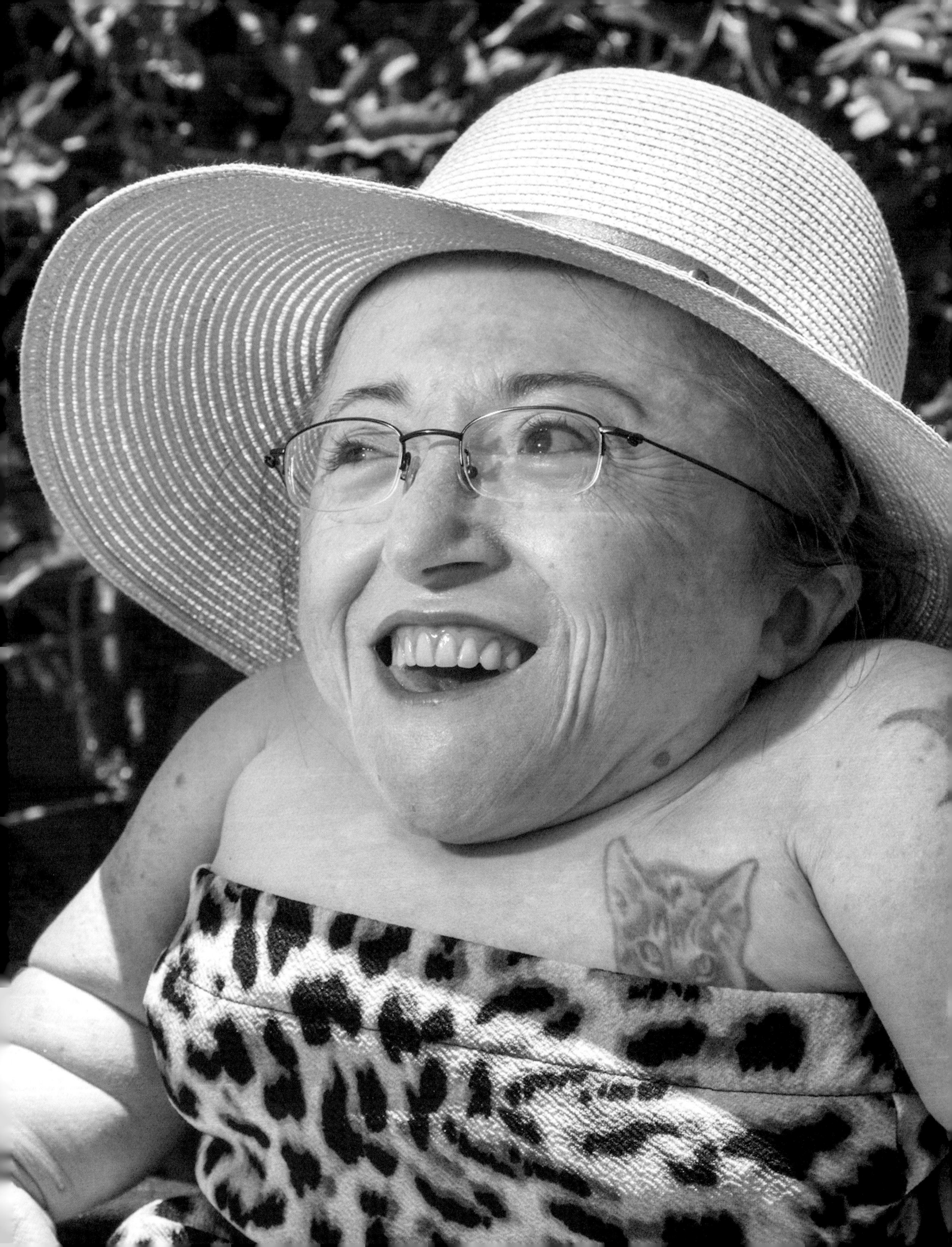

Jane Hash

Jane was born in a small town in Ohio. She was diagnosed almost immediately with osteogenesis imperfecta, a brittle bone disease. In fact, she was born with skull fractures and bone fractures that were not able to be set.

At the time that she was born, little was known about this disease, and her mother was told that Jane wouldn't survive, and that if she did, she ought to be put in a nursing facility. Thankfully, neither of these things happened and her mother took her home.

Jane went to public school in Ohio, and while she faced some challenges, she was supported by her mother. As Jane had brittle bones, holding and using heavy textbooks wasn't possible for her. Jane was able to advocate for herself when she experienced barriers, such as a step that prevented her from going onto the playground in her wheelchair. In terms of her connections with others, Jane felt included in school and had friends and peer support.

"There was no plan for me."

After high school, Jane had to find her own next step, and wanting to go to college to study business, she reached out and found support. Through home care programs, she was able to put her own system in place so that she could travel to and take classes at the local community college. Unfortunately, this vanished when the home care program was taken over by another managed care system.

Following a brief move to Michigan (too cold!), Jane decided that the central coast of California was where she wanted to be. While Jane would like to be paid for all of the work that she does, she is constrained by a system that only allows her to earn $700 per month. If she earns more, she is no longer eligible to receive her medical equipment and the support of her caregivers.

"Eight hundred dollars a month doesn't pay for your care. This rule doesn't make sense unless the goal is to keep you trapped."

Today, Jane is healthy and has established a network of friends who keep her connected and encourage her advocacy work. She has worked as a blogger, hosted a radio show, and entertained as a mermaid.

She continues to push for disability rights and inclusion and believes that a new approach needs to be taken. Attempting to secure disability rights the way that we have been is not the most effective strategy. Disability advocates need to be seen in all spaces, ensuring that corporations understand the value of including people with disabilities in the workforce.

Poem Origin Story

When we meet, Jane is dressed in a black and white, tiger striped, off the shoulder shirt. I can see her pentagram tattoo, which she mentions later is a symbol of her willingness to chart her own course and be true to herself. It's also one of the things that she says gets people's attention.

It is clear in our conversation that Jane is deeply thoughtful about her own development and about her connections with others. She values the people in her life and knows that, out of necessity, she has to rely on them.

While she is immensely grateful to those who help her, she feels like it's sometimes been easy for her to fall into a trap of feeling that as a result of their help, she's beholden to them and does what they want her to do. She's been able to reset this thinking and has stayed true to herself by making the choices that are best for her.

I asked her about her identity, and she replied that because her disability is obvious, she doesn't pretend that it's not there. At the same time, it's not what she leads with.

Jane values her autonomy and agency and is always striving to grow and meet her full potential—sometimes pushing against rules and systems that make this hard for people with disabilities.

She hopes that the example that she provides by living her life openly and as she chooses will help others to do the same.

Unapologetically, Me

We may think
That mermaids hide,
Choosing the deep.
Elusive.
Not wanting to be seen.

But those
Who live in our world
Are bold.
They claim themselves-
Tails or toes
Land and sea.
Unapologetically.

This one
Has no lack of confidence...
"They're going to notice me anyway!"
She declares,
Choosing
Colorful
Clothes and poses.
Radiating joy from the inside out.

She recognizes her limitations,
Finding strength
In the boundaries and borderlines,
And in her repeated crossings.

It's only her belly-button,
She says,
That betrays her.
Proving that she's a land dweller,
Not from the sea.

This mermaid, however, requires help,
Relying on others
For what she can't do
Herself.

Grateful for those who care for her,
Though her gratitude
Looks like
Autonomy.
As she works
To meet
Her full potential.

It's safe-
Follow this mermaid
into
The water.

Nicole Demos

Nicole and her family were living in Greece, and her parents were told that they had two choices: throw this baby in the garbage or put her in an asylum. Since then, the road has been filled with challenges and victories. Her family returned to the United States, where Nicole was diagnosed with cerebral palsy, specifically spastic diplegia. Here, her family learned about the care that Nicole would require, including physical therapy, and any future treatments and medical equipment that she might need, such as crutches and a wheelchair. In spite of some disagreement from family members, her family then returned home to Greece where Nicole lived until she was eighteen.

Living in Greece was challenging, as there were few services for Nicole and her parents. She felt like the attitude was, "How dare my parents take me out in public." In Athens, Nicole was able to attend American community schools on scholarship until graduation, and despite this being the best option for her, she still experienced teasing, isolation, and bullying.

"I thought of myself as a burden."

Nicole then attended the University of Hartford, earning her BS in special education. She had expected life to be easier in the United States but found herself facing challenges because the environment was not accessible. She also believed that she would have many opportunities for employment but was told on several occasions that while she was qualified for the job, as a result of her disability, she was believed to be a liability.

Nonetheless, Nicole has worked as an educator in a variety of settings. Her professional roles range from working at a residential facility for behaviorally challenged students to creating a learning support program at a school

"I advocated for my students in a way that I never did for myself."

in Moscow and later to online teaching. Along the way, she also earned two master's degrees.

In March of 2023, while on a trip to Greece to give a keynote speech at the school that she had attended, Nicole got sick. Due to the poor care that she received en route to the airport medical center, she stopped breathing, had to be resuscitated, and spent eleven days in the lung ward. Upon her return to Helsinki, Nicole continued to have traumatic experiences through the poor care she received. Her CP has become more pronounced, and she has developed arthritis, sleep apnea, sciatica, and depression.

Despite these challenges, she continues to forge ahead, working as a disability educator and advocate, and making connections with others across the world. Nicole has recently become a Certified Listener Poet and has given her first TED talk.

Poem Origin Story

When we begin our conversation, it's clear that Nicole is in a place of struggle. For a person with a physical disability, finding a home that is comfortable and accessible is critical, and Nicole is having to work on finding such a place. It's a hard spot to be in, but she wants to forge ahead with our conversation, nonetheless.

In the past two or three years, Nicole has proudly identified as a disabled person. Prior to that, she chose not to see herself as, nor to call herself, disabled. She wanted to be like everyone else and didn't want to have accommodations. She felt frustration and anger that there wasn't a system in place to ensure her access. It was upsetting that she had to fight to go places and to be a part of something. She hadn't yet learned to advocate for herself.

A few years ago, she found power in her voice and now openly claims her disability. She's come to peace with who she is. Nicole has been able to do away with the what ifs and is able to focus on the things that move her as a person. She holds on to the connections that she has and the moments of joy and fulfillment.

The Cloud of What-Ifs

What if
...I get there and can't do it.
...I need help.
...I'm not strong enough.
...I feel sorry for myself.
...I'm different from others.
...They ignore me.
...I'm in pain.
...They talk down to me.
...They don't see me.

I'm alone.

What if
...I can be strong.
...I bubble over with excitement.
...My angst is gone.
...I don't have to pretend not to be in
pain.
...I can fight for myself.
...It's okay to ask for help.
...I have people who support me.
...People know me for who I am.
...People care about me.
...My voice is powerful.

I'm still here.

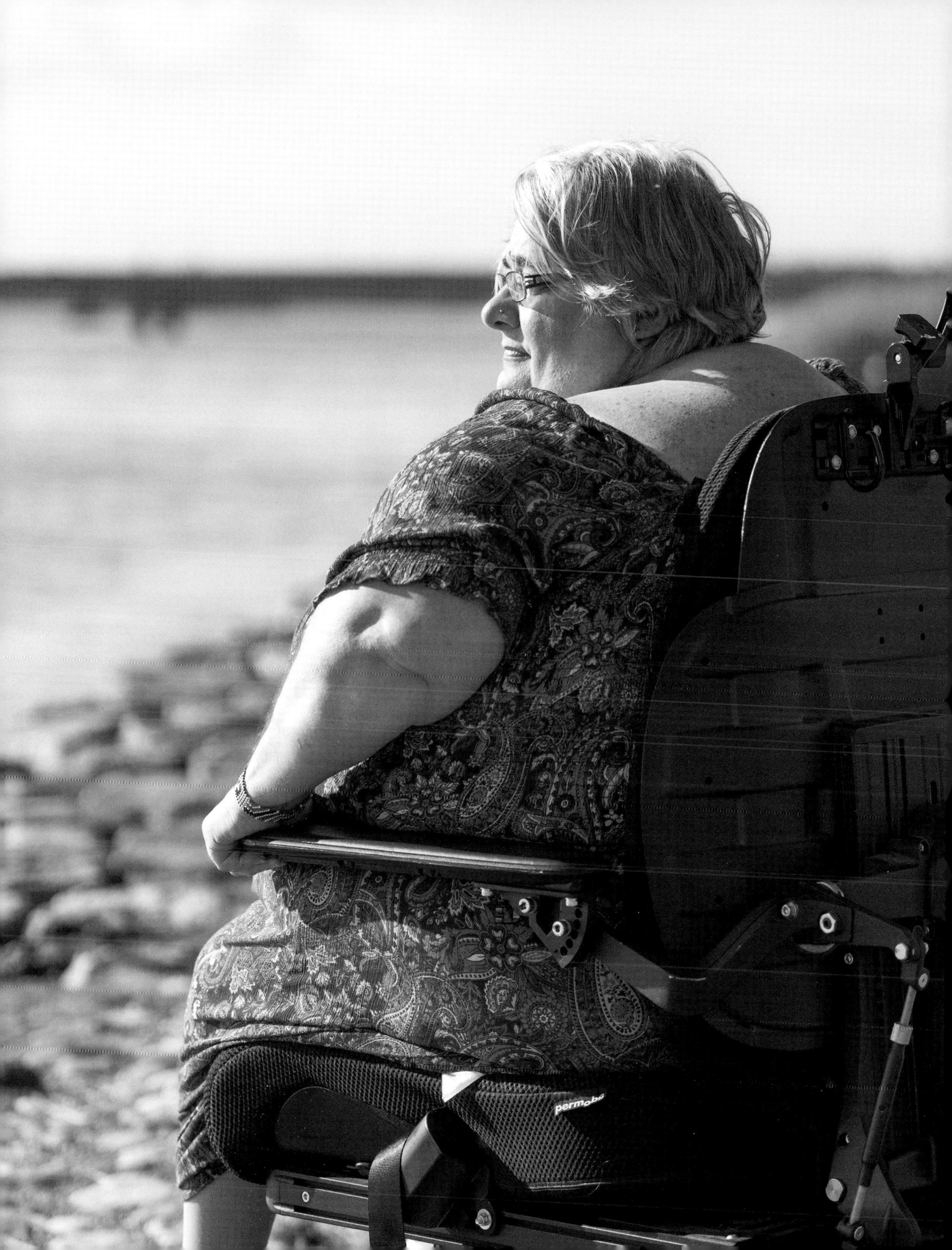

Trevor Hahn

Trevor was born and raised in Fort Collins, Colorado, and has always had a love of the outdoors. In spite of his poor vision, he was an active, artistic child, and has grown into an adult who continues to pursue design and sculpture and who travels and climbs across the world.

As a child, Trevor experienced vision challenges and was very nearsighted. This meant that he had to wear thick, high prescription glasses and that his vision became worse as he got older. In high school, Trevor developed inflammation in his eyes that further compromised his vision. For a while, this inflammation and cloudiness seemed to impact only one eye at a time, so he was still able to see.

It was at the end of high school that one of Trevor's retinas detached and he had to have surgery to reattach it. He ended up losing sight in one of his eyes and experiencing uveitis, inflammation, in the other eye.

Nonetheless, Trevor went to college, first attending Fort Lewis College and then graduating from Colorado State University with a degree in fine art and a concentration in graphic design.

It wasn't until after he graduated from college that he was diagnosed with ankylosing spondylitis, a form of autoimmune arthritis that impacts the spine and vision.

As he was still experiencing eye inflammation, he was glad to find an advertising job in Arizona that allowed him to work from home. After a few years working in Arizona (too hot!), Trevor returned to Colorado and found work with a brewery that hired him to do their branding and advertising design.

Back home, Trevor returned to the outdoor activities that he loved; he connected with No Barriers and Paradox Sports and began to rock climb and ice climb. He also was able to travel—backpacking in Europe, New Zealand, and Nepal. In 2014, the pressure in Trevor's eyes got so high that it damaged his optic nerve and his sight never returned.

"Losing my sight meant that I was cut off from art and the outdoors. What do I do now?"

For a while, Trevor was unsure of what to do next. It wasn't until he found a fundraiser for the Fort Collins Museum of Art that entailed designing a mask that would be sold to benefit the museum that Trevor became inspired, wanting to create something to show the experience of losing his sight. He created a mask called "Igniting from the Darkness," which he calls a self portrait with flames coming from the eyes.

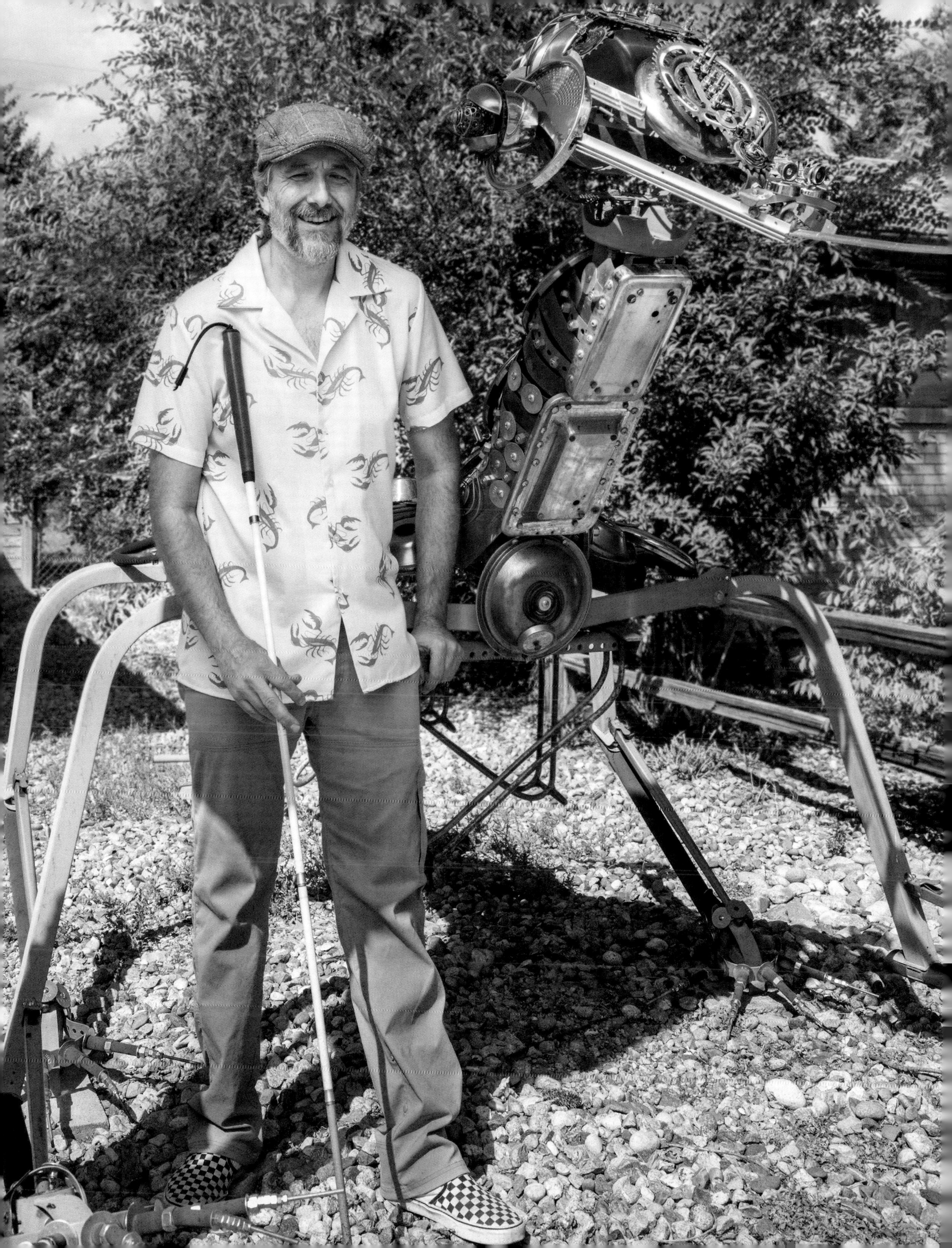

"If I can feel the form, I can create."

This experience inspired Trevor to revisit sculpture, and he created Trevor Hahn's Art Through Touch. He now creates whimsical, industrial pieces, recycling materials including metal and wood in his art and sculptures. His work is done by drilling and fastening pieces rather than welding them.

In addition to dedicating time to his art, Trevor has fallen in love with climbing again. Because climbing is tactile, he's able to use his hands and feet to "trad climb," following the crack up the rock face. Trevor has also taken up ice climbing which allows him to use crampons and climbing tools to traverse the frozen rock.

Thus, in both his art and his climbing, Trevor uses senses other than sight to engage with tactile forms.

Poem Origin Story

Because Trevor lived much of his early life with sight, it's difficult for him to say with conviction that he thinks of himself as a person with a disability. When he lost his sight fully, he did initially feel like he had a disability, at least insofar as the world around him was suddenly inaccessible. He felt seen and treated as a person with a disability, but as he learned to adapt, Trevor didn't see himself this way; he was just a person who found other ways to do things.

When he lost his sight, Trevor found other ways to do the things that he loved. He discovered what he calls "superpowers," which are the skills and senses that he has other than his sight. He hears better than he had and is aware of sounds that he probably wouldn't have noticed when he could see.

Trevor's memory, especially his spatial memory, has improved leaps and bounds. He has an exceptionally well organized tool bench and shop and relies on his memory and sense of touch to create, develop, and build the pieces that he makes. He also uses this spatial sense to store and find his tools and materials so that he can easily access them.

Trevor feels that his blindness has been the motivation to do bigger, greater things than he would have done if he hadn't lost his sight. His objectives include breaking any barriers that might be in the way of him doing all that he wants to do.

Blind Sight

My ears
And hands
Have become my eyes.
And in this way,
I see
Better than
You do.

Attentive
To the quietest sound
In the forest
Or on the street.

Sounds that
Your ears miss.

Aware
Of how the asphalt, sidewalk,
grass, and meadow
Feel
Under my feet,
And at the tip of my cane.

I have memories
Of the places I've been
And make fast memories
Of the places I go;
Mental maps that guide me.

I can choose
The right item
Out of the cabinet-
I've memorized the shape, size, and
texture of its packaging.

I can find
The smallest bolt, washer, or thread
On my workbench;
Can build bees, butterflies, spiders,
and scorpions.
Seeing them
Inside my head.

In these ways,
I see
So much more
Than what my eyes
Alone
Might show me.

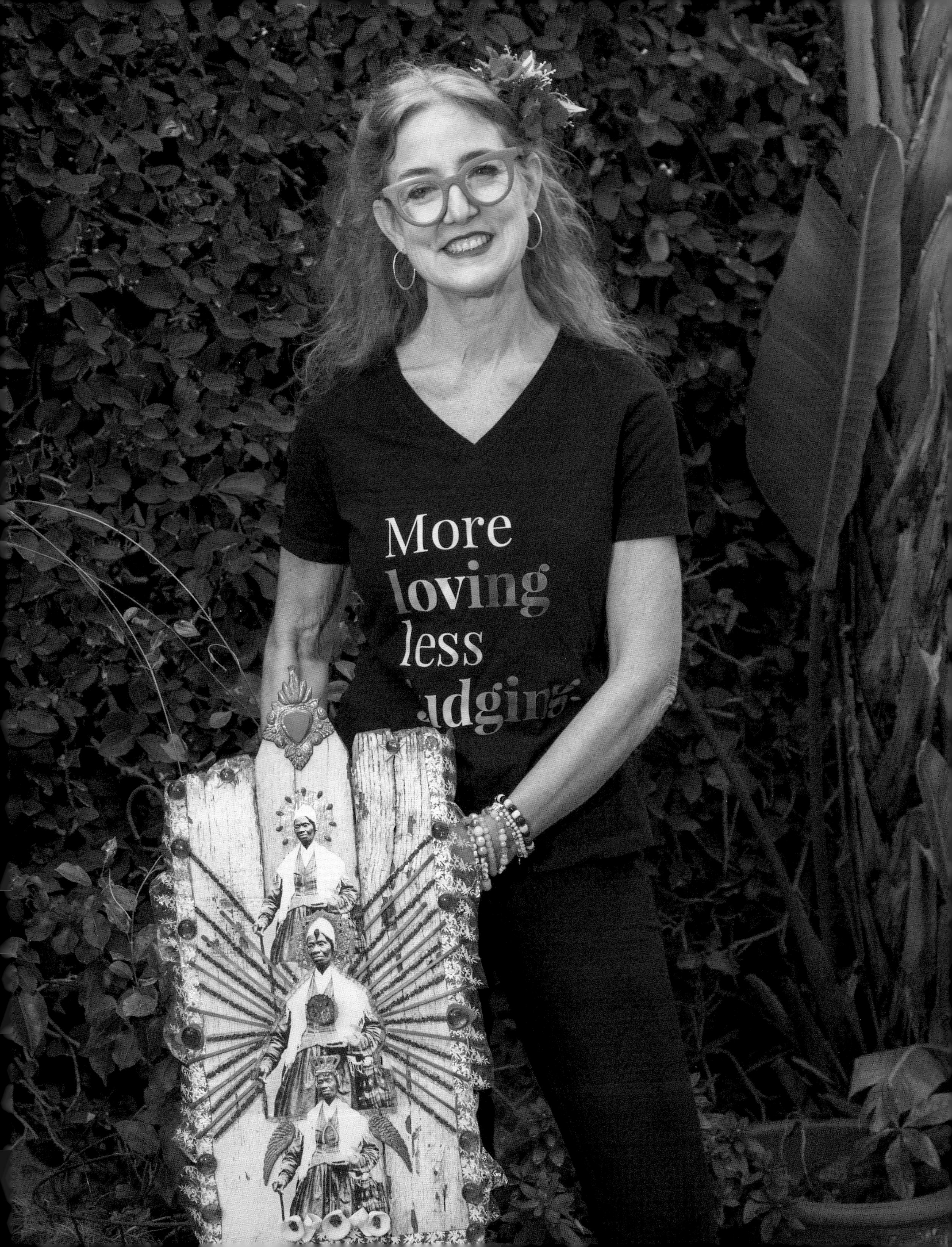
More
loving
less

Hope Demetriades

Hope has wanted to be a ballerina her whole life. Initially as a child, she found joy in her dancing, in spite of the fact that sometimes positions were painful for her. She unwittingly hyperextended her legs, and fixing her position felt uncomfortable. Additionally, as a result of her dyslexia, she sometimes mistook her right for her left and felt shame when she was called out for it.

In high school, Hope had some heart and hip pain but brushed it off and was active in spite of it. It wasn't until she experienced so much pain while dancing that it also caused pain off stage in her everyday activities, that she finally accepted the fact that she would not be able to dance professionally.

Hope lived most of her life without a diagnosis of Ehlers Danlos syndrome (EDS). It was only when her second son was born, and he was diagnosed with Ehlers Danlos, that she too was diagnosed as having it. Part of the lack of diagnosis was a result of Hope being active and being encouraged to simply push through the pain when she experienced it.

As a result of the EDS, Hope experiences chronic connective tissue and joint pain, has an irregular heartbeat, and has painful sciatica. She also has herniated discs and has had to have several hip surgeries.

When she was a child, Hope was bussed to schools in LA and changed schools each year. While this was hard for her as she was very shy, she credits these experiences with helping her to feel comfortable with those who were different from her. Most of her classmates were students of color, and her experiences with them made her sensitized to injustice.

Much of Hope's professional work as an artist has been focused on the canonizing of American abolitionists. She began this work when Obama was elected because she felt the need to acknowledge and call attention to the fact that there was

"In spite of the fact that I walk and don't look like I have a disability, I'm in pain every day."

"You don't get to participate in the world the way that most people do when you are made to feel othered."

still much work to do before we could claim that we were living in a "post racial world."

Having a disability has led to her having empathy for others, which has led to her becoming an activist, artist, and educator. Being disabled is hard, but it has been quadruply hard for her to experience her kids being othered and excluded due to their differences.

Poem Origin Story

For much of her life, Hope dismissed the pain and discomfort that she experienced, not realizing that they were indicators of a genetic disorder that impacted her ability to be fully active and to live without pain. It was only in adulthood that she was finally diagnosed with Ehlers Danlos syndrome and began to think of herself as a person with a disability.

In the process of coming to see herself as a person with a disability, and often an invisible one, Hope's concept and understanding of disability has changed. This recognition of invisible disabilities has Hope asking herself, "How many people are walking around this world with hidden disabilities?"

Hope struggles with the fact that she is able to do less than she wants to and less than she could do in the past. She is a dancer and has always been active. Now she can't run, can't surf, and can't dance. Hope has found herself asking, "How will I actually live with this kind of pain every day?" She's found herself answering by turning to the tough kid that she was raised to be and moving forward.

Tough/Fragile

This vessel,
So easily breakable
And yet,
unbroken.

Dressed
In a body
That appears;
Strong,
Whole,
Steady.

You assume
That I
Can
Do more
Than I really can.
Making me feel
Like I should
Shoulder
More weight
Than I can bear.

I believe this too-
Have been taught to believe it.

Until,
I can't.
One day, tough.
The next day, fragile.

In my shyness,
I never ask
For the
Help
That I need.

Instead,
Hiding
Joints
Like Japanese Kintsugi.
Their breaks,
tough/fragile,
Fuel
My fire.

My heart and head
Want so badly to say, "yes."
But my body
Declines
Your invitation.
Please don't stop asking.

Jacob Lesner Buxton

Jacob was diagnosed with cerebral palsy (CP) when he was born in Oakland, California. At this time, it was often believed that a person who had CP would not be able to walk, talk, and lead a "typical" life. Fortunately, Jacob had a mother who knew better and treated Jacob as she would any other child, having high expectations for him and supporting him as he grew. She also insisted that anyone who came to visit their home treated Jacob as they would anyone else.

"My mom was told that I wouldn't be able to walk or to talk and that I'd spend my life in a wheelchair."

Jacob's family and many family friends were also involved in the disability rights movement, so Jacob has participated in rallies since he was a child. He attended school alongside his peers for his whole life. In high school at Far West School, Jacob found his niche, learning about social justice and getting his start as a public speaker. Here, he attended his first conference for high school students with disabilities and fell in love with disability rights organizing. It was also at this time that Jacob first identified as Queer, though he felt that he had to hide this part of his identity because homophobia existed in the disability community. Later, when he saw disability advocates claiming their Queer identity, he felt safe doing so as well.

"I didn't really identify with disability until my senior year of high school."

After high school, he attended California State University, Monterey Bay, earning a BA in health and human services, and then went on to earn a master's degree in social work from California State University, East Bay. Soon after earning his degrees, Jacob began working for the Independent Living Resource Center (now Access Central Coast) as a systems change coordinator. He has been in this role for eleven and a half years, working with people with disabilities across the central coast of California. In 2023, Jacob met and married his wife, Chelsea, who also worked at ILRC.

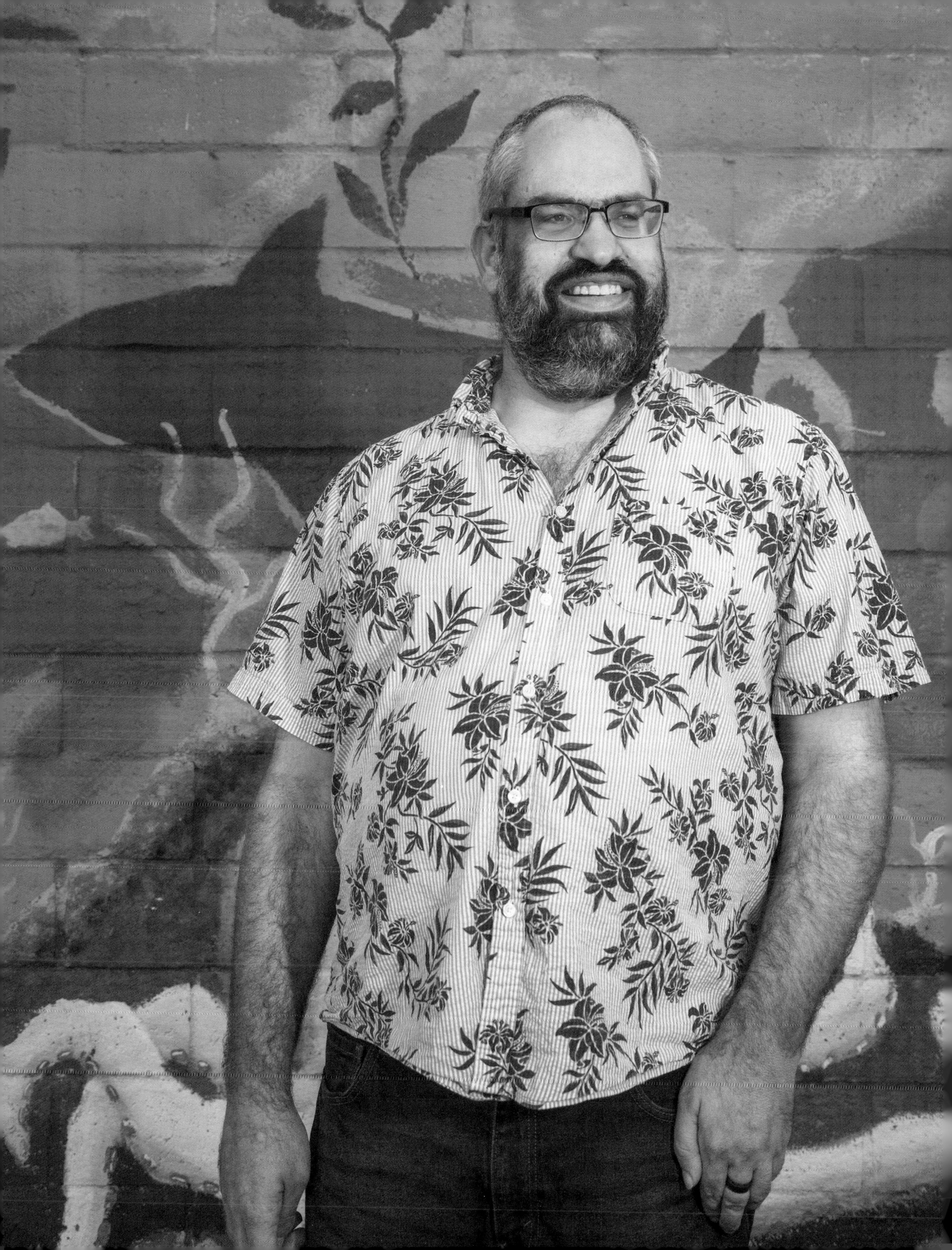

In spite of his successes, Jacob still feels the impact of being a person with a disability. He has struggled to get the health care that he needs and says that he can't bring other people with him to appointments with health care professionals because often they speak to the person that he brought with him, rather than speaking to him. He works in his personal and professional life to combat exclusion and ableism of this sort.

Poem Origin Story

When he was four or five years old, Jacob told his mother that he wished that he didn't have cerebral palsy. He doesn't feel this way anymore and has come to accept his disease and to appreciate what he can do.

Jacob's disability is obvious, and even if he wanted to, he can't hide it. As a result, he's had to decide how to respond to the remarks that people make and actions that they take. Too often, people make assumptions that Jacob is being taken care of by someone else, that he is a child, or that he lacks cognitive capacity. For the most part, he's able to laugh off these comments and interactions.

Jacob has chosen to respond with humor and has created a t shirt that has his résumé on it. He wears it when he's out and about and especially when he goes to the doctor's office so that people understand that he's accomplished.

The frustrations that Jacob feels with his life tend to be related to simple tasks like having to forgo his orange juice because he can't open the cap. He also feels some frustration in trying to be understood with his speech impediment; sometimes it's hard enough for him to be understood that he and the person that he's talking to decide just to move on without clarity and this makes both of them feel bad.

Despite his challenges, Jacob approaches life thinking that these awkward moments will ultimately make good stories.

Same As

When I told
My mother
I didn't want
To have Cerebral Palsy,
She said,
"You'll learn how to deal with it
Later."
And I have...
Have you?

I'm disabled
Can't change that.
It's obvious,
Can't hide it.

What you don't see;
I've lived independently for 15 years,
Earned a Master's Degree in Social Work.
I have a job,
And a wife.
I can afford the bill,
And even add a tip.

A unique
individual.
And yet,
I'm often mistaken
For other disabled people...
Because we all look alike, right?
I've learned to just laugh-
These will be good stories
To tell.

Please
Don't talk to me
Like I'm a child.

Don't ignore me.

I look
And sound
Different than you do.

But
I'm here
And whole
And capable
And kind.

My voice is hard to understand
It takes effort,
I know.
I know
That I'm doing my best.
Won't you do
Your best
To understand?

Dr. Arielle Dance

Dr. Dance is a left-handed only child from New Jersey. She grew up in a multi-generational home with her grandparents, her mother, and her mother's siblings. She enjoyed school and felt connected to her church. As a child and a teenager, Arielle enjoyed performing arts, riding horses, and cheerleading. In college at Spelman, she was part of a touring glee club. In her adulthood, she has returned to dancing and become re-engaged with community theatre. Even as a child, she was a writer, an avocation that she would carry into adulthood.

When Arielle was fifteen years old, she was diagnosed with endometriosis, a debilitating and painful disease in which tissue similar to the lining of the uterus grows outside of the uterus. As a result of this tissue growth, she had to have six surgeries over the next twenty years, including having her uterus removed when she was thirty three years old. Because of her chronic pain, she sometimes struggles to be able to do the basic tasks of daily living and self-care.

Arielle has also had two incidents of pulmonary embolism, blood clots in her lungs. This medical condition can be life-threatening and must be carefully managed by taking medication, choosing healthy foods, and being exceedingly cautious when traveling—especially when flying.

During college, Arielle acknowledged and claimed her disability. She chose to live in accessible housing and met other students with disabilities. She experienced a feeling of acceptance in this community, knowing that others had struggled with the same pain and the same misunderstandings as she had.

In college and in graduate school, Arielle chose to study women's health. In fact, her master's thesis and her doctoral dissertation both focused on endometriosis. Her work at the American Cancer Society (ACS) allows her to design and advocate for community programs designed to care for those living with and surviving cancer. She is a leader of the disability focused employee resource group.

"I was asked by a counselor who worked with the disabled students, 'How are you today?' You realize that nobody has asked you that since you left home."

"I would not have gone to the hospital if I hadn't heard your story."

When she's not working at ACS, Arielle is a writer. She is a children's book author, a poet, and, since 2022, a writer for Diversability, a disability organization. In all of these spaces, she works to amplify the stories of people with disabilities. She shows up by storytelling, wanting to let people know that they are not alone in their struggles. As part of this effort, she often speaks about her illnesses and writes for other organizations. She has been told that she's saved people's lives by sharing her story.

Poem Origin Story

At some times in her life, Arielle has struggled with the idea of defining herself as disabled, as she felt like she might not "deserve" the identity. Her illness, one that was and continues to be disabling, was invisible. She wondered if her disabling condition was somehow different enough from being blind, deaf, or using a wheelchair that she shouldn't claim it, shouldn't define it as a disability.

She's grown to understand that disabilities come in a variety of manifestations. Some are invisible; some come and go, sometimes visible and disabling and at other times invisible and less impactful. That said, other people's perceptions impact our choices about our self identification. As Arielle has grown to feel comfortable claiming her disability, she's heard from others with invisible disabilities who appreciate her willingness to say that she is disabled, as it helps them to feel that they can do so as well.

Before her hysterectomy two years ago, Arielle was in pain daily and had about one good week each month. Though she's in less pain now, she's able to recall that past pain and the challenges that came with it.

As a result of the care that she had, and that she knows is not available for everyone, Arielle is left with a feeling of gratitude. She's had the best medical care, an encouraging family, and loving caregivers. She feels that in spite of the hard times, she is not left with anger or fear, but only appreciation for getting to where she is now.

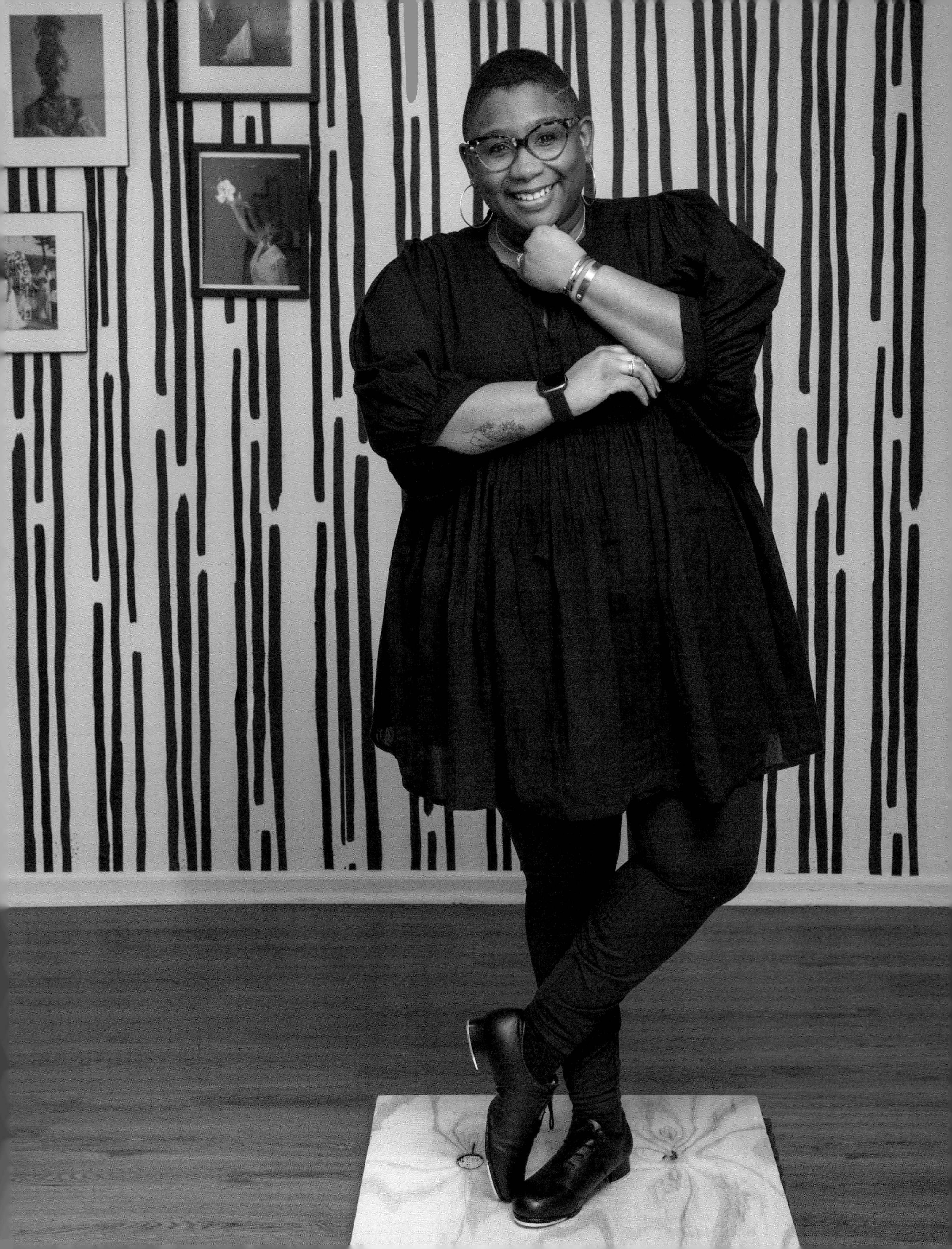

And Still, They Pick Me Up.

I'm left with this
Faint,
But indelible
Memory.

Just enough awareness-
My mother,
Brushing my hair;
My wife
Brushing my teeth.
I lay
Loosely,
holding on
To consciousness
In the hospital bed.

Even if I don't recall it,
I know
That I felt better
For their care.

I needed them
To pick me up
To hold me up.

They know
And accept-

That even though
Dancing
Causes me pain,
I'd rather do it,
Paying for it later,
Than miss out
On the joy that it brings.

And still,
They pick me up.

I am draped in gratitude,
Wearing it wherever I go.

Dominick Trevethan

Dominick credits his father for always having high expectations for him. It is because of these expectations, and the care that he received from his father and his grandparents, that Dominick is where he is today.

When he was eight months old, Dominick was not yet crawling. He was assessed and diagnosed with spinal muscular atrophy, a degenerative genetic condition that is marked by a lack of the gene that is responsible for motor neuron growth.

Because he was encouraged, Dominick didn't accept complacency and has always pushed himself to pursue his goals. When his school district wanted to place him in special education classes, Dominick and his father challenged this placement and Dominick was placed in traditional classes. Here, he thrived, taking honors and AP classes and attending University of California, Los Angeles (UCLA).

While he left UCLA after two years, Dominick had a better understanding of what he needed to be successful, and being at home was beneficial for him. He went on to earn an associate's degree from Hancock College and then a BS in communications from Arizona State University.

Part of the challenge that Dominick has faced is getting reliable nursing care, which he needs around the clock. There is a lack of reliable nursing care, and this is compounded by the fact that the insured rate for paying nurses is very low. His most reliable caregiver only makes $17 per hour. He has missed classes and been late to final exams because his nurses failed to show. He relies on them and can't go anywhere without this care.

After college, Dominick was interested in public speaking and was encouraged to create a podcast to showcase his skills. Thus, The Disability Myth was born.

Through this podcast, Dominick has focused on advocating for others and breaking down misconceptions about disability.

"When I could no longer raise my hand in class, my father taped an American flag to a ruler, and I could just tip this up when I wanted to participate."

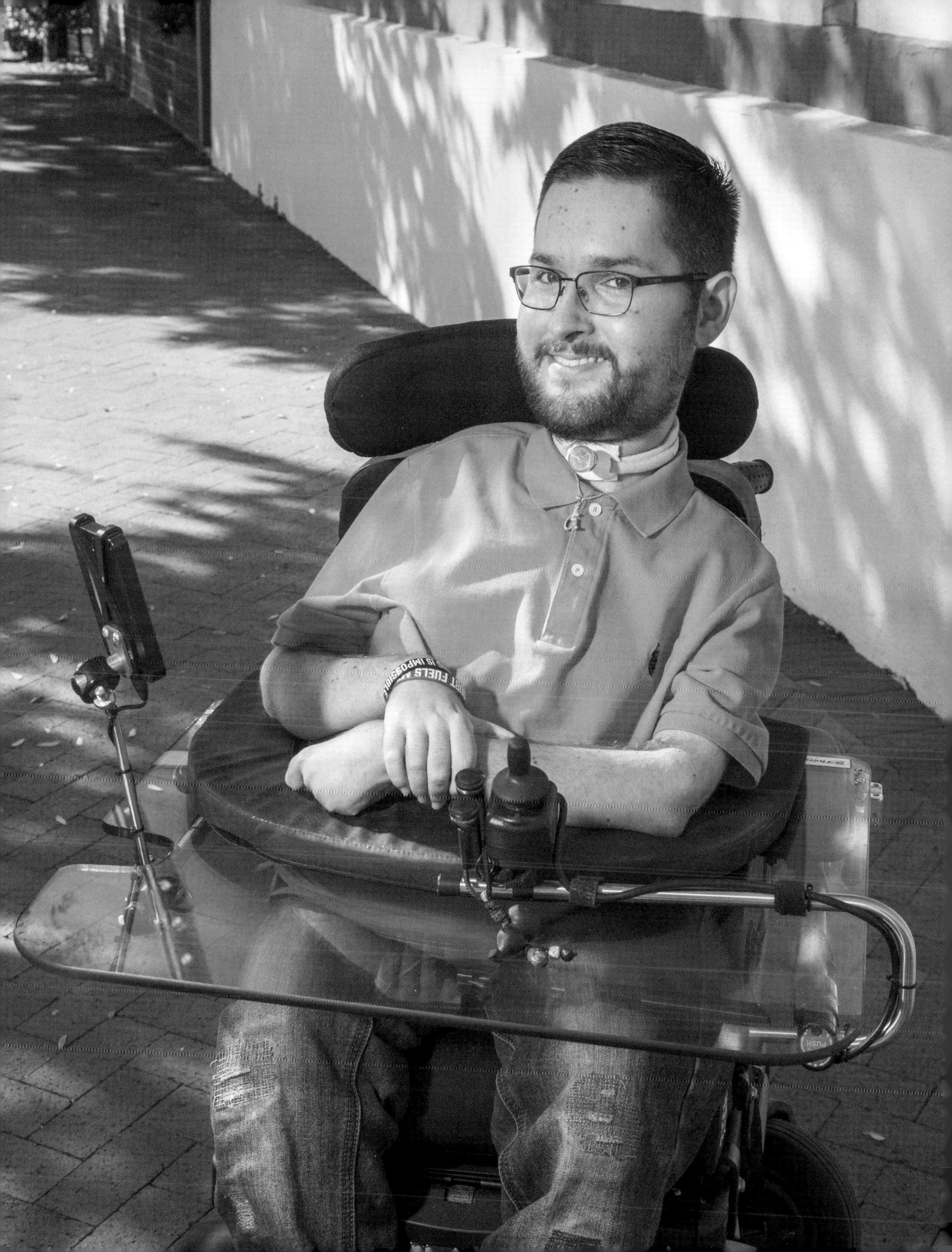

"I try to create stories that resonate with everyone, so that people can better connect to and understand people with disabilities."

The podcast has also led to the opportunity to work as the producer and editor for Pushing Limits, a radio show that raises awareness of issues and challenges that those in the disability community face.

In addition to this work, Dominick contracts with Cottage Rehabilitation Hospital. Here, he coordinates and hosts virtual wheelchair sports camps and organizes monthly presentations for people with disabilities who have been through the Cottage Hospital rehabilitation program.

Poem Origin Story

As a communications major, words matter to Dominick. He describes his journey from defining himself as a disabled person to identifying as a person with a disability as a process of becoming who he wants to be. When he was young, he felt that he had a lot to be afraid of. Specifically, he was told that he wouldn't live past thirty years of age. As he's grown older, he's realized that he can live a full and fulfilling life. This realization has helped him to make the decision to own his disability, but to do so in a way that puts his personhood first.

Dominick recognizes that, out of necessity, he must rely on others for his care. While he sometimes worries about being a burden and sometimes notices signs of frustration that caregivers may unintentionally display when he asks for something that he needs, he feels fortunate that his caregivers have been so committed to his health, safety, and comfort.

Out of necessity, Dominick and sometimes his caregivers have to be focused on logistics and have to overthink, overplan, and overcommunicate in order to navigate the world. In relying on others, Dominick has learned to live with vulnerability and has developed a maturity that enables him to advocate for the parts of himself that he hadn't previously valued and honored.

A Billion Little Things

A billion
Little things
That people
Think about and say to me;

He must not be smart
He's trapped in that chair
He's not productive
Not educated
Stays home all day
He doesn't contribute to the world
Doesn't have a job

They're so wrong.

A billion
Little things
That run
Through my head each day;

Minute details, and
Critical information.

Have I slept well?
Do I have the energy...
        To get out of bed?
        To hold myself up?
Can't forget to:
        Do my breathing treatments
        Call the doctor
        Call the pharmacy

Respond to emails
Volunteer
Coach at adaptive sports camp
Write, edit, and record my podcasts
Plan new podcasts
Contact guests

I barely find time to rest.

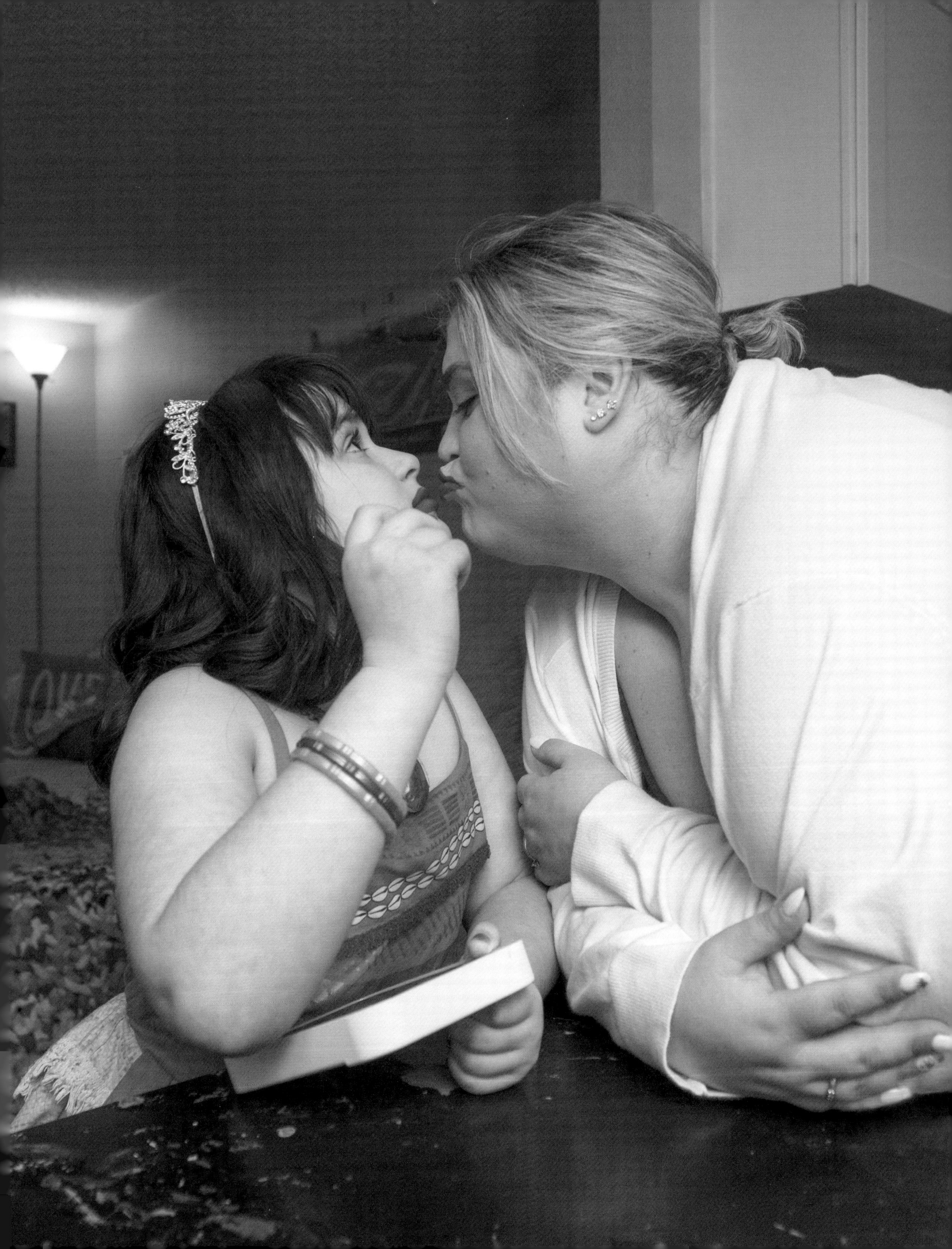

Cassie and Hailey Enea

When Cassie gave birth to her daughter, Hailey, she was excited to have, as she called her, a "perfect little pinto bean."

Her pregnancy with Hailey had been a hard one, as she had experienced several false labors and feared, on multiple occasions, that her baby would come too early. When she did come, she was breech and was delivered by cesarean section.

While she was small, Hailey seemed to be growing well and was hitting all of her developmental milestones. At nine months of age, she began talking, and by one year, she was walking.

It seemed to Cassie that a sudden change took place with Hailey just after her first birthday. She no longer walked on her own, and her talking became nearly non-existent. She was found to have ear infections, and had tubes placed in her ears. This treatment initially seemed to address the changes in her walking and talking, as she began to do both again. Unfortunately, this was a brief change. By the time she was one and a half, she was only moving by walking unsteadily, crawling upstairs, and had virtually stopped talking again.

"I am her voice, and she is my heart."

Soon after this, Cassie was encouraged to take Hailey to be tested for autism. When she was two and a half years old, Hailey was diagnosed with autism spectrum disorder, level three (level four is the most severe). Additionally, she was found to have an intellectual delay.

For Hailey, school has also been a challenge, as not all schools are well-equipped to meet her needs. She is now attending a school that provides an inclusive and specialized curriculum to students who have intellectual and developmental disabilities. She's much happier in this school setting.

"I find myself grieving the life that she could have had."

In spite of the fact that Hailey is not a "typical" kid, she understands a lot of what is happening and has her own ways of communicating. She also likes dancing and sports.

Adding to the challenges that Cassie faces is her own diagnosis of lupus, as a result of which she experiences chronic pain and brain fog. Nonetheless, she is deeply dedicated to her daughter and hopes for her to live a joyous life.

Poem Origin Story

My conversation with Hailey requires that her mother, Cassie, be there as well. As we begin, Cassie calls Hailey over to talk with me. It turns out that Cassie has told Hailey that after our conversation they can go get some tea, so that is what Hailey is thinking about. When she sits down, she says, "Tea, tea, tea."

Throughout our conversation, Hailey is up and down, stepping away and then returning with a handheld microphone, and later with bright red lipstick generously applied to her lips and mouth.

It is clear that she understands much of what I ask and what Cassie repeats, because her actions match our questions and comments, though her verbal responses are limited. For some of the time that we're talking, Hailey is on the floor organizing her princess coins and looking at her books, which she shows me when I ask about them.

Reengaging with me requires prompting from Cassie, but when we're about to end the call, Hailey gets up and comes over to say goodbye.

Her Humanity

On walks, she collects acorns-
Seeds of possibility-
Smooth and soothing,
Carried home for tea parties,
Organized and well-thought out.
Carefully arranged
On plates for nibbling.

This world
Sometimes too much;
So many sounds,
So many people.
Covering her ears, closing her eyes,
She grabs ahold
Of what makes sense to her.

She looks
Like the child that she is.

Until, and until, and until
She talks.
Repeating
Book, book, book
Coco, coco, coco,
Go, go, go.
Staccato words come from her lips,
She's stuck in a loop,
Hyper Fixated,
Focused.
Finally, the need is met,
And she can let go.

Until, and until, and until
She puts on her lipstick;
Bright red lips,
Drawn with a child's hand
Increasing and accentuating
Her open mouth.

She walks away
From the questions
For which she doesn't have answers.

Since she was born, there have been
many questions.
And fewer answers.

Day by day.
It's hard to see the future,
But easy to see,
To re-see,
The world
Through her eyes.

We are left,
Waiting for what's next.
Wondering
What she makes of this world,
What she will make in this world.
Responding to our words,
But having few of her own.
Her body engaged,
Dancing, running, silent singing.
Laying with mama when she needs to rest.

Poem Origin Story

In our conversation, Steven described "trying to bury as much as he could" of his hearing loss when he was young. He wanted to be able-bodied because it seemed to him that only able-bodied people were successful, a message that he had taken in from the world around him. He sometimes felt that he wasn't enough. People like him weren't celebrated.

For Steven, every day is a day that he has to conquer fear. Being DeafBlind can be scary. When he can't hear, he can't communicate and thus, feels isolated. With the confidence that he's gained and the aids that he can rely on, Steven has become a "conversation starter," willing to extend himself to connect with others.

As he's gotten older, Steven has grown to be more accepting of himself. He knows that when he, and others with disabilities, enter into any room, they're bringing a different and original perspective. He often finds that people's experiences are both unique and universal, and this allows for growth and learning, as well as connection. He hopes that we all as humans can embrace differences, step out of our boxes, do more, be more, and try something new.

To Be a Part of the World

I didn't know who to be.
Didn't know when to be.
Will I be enough?

There's hesitation,
Preparation;
Should I go out?
Who will be there?
Will I feel safe?

I'm not the way that I used to be,
It's not the way that it used to
be.

The photograph in front of me –
I haven't been that person
For so long.

To be a part
Of the world.
Not apart
From the world.
Requires a willingness –
Risk.
To shed
Yesterday's skin
That holds us back.
To trust
That someone
Will meet us,
As we are,
When we
Enter.

Steven McCoy

While Steven has been able to maintain a joyful spirit, he characterized his childhood as a lonely, isolated time in his life. He vividly recalls the test that his mother conducted when he was five years old. Evidently, after spending the day playing outside, he hadn't been coming in in the evening when he and the other kids were called. Because he wasn't the sort to ignore his mother calling to him, she had become concerned and wanted to check his hearing. She had Steven and his brothers go into a back room in the house and called each one. Steven never heard his name being called, and when he came out, she asked him if he had heard his name. He had not. This led to testing and a diagnosis that Steven was deaf.

"I never saw anyone like me being celebrated...on TV or in magazines."

Despite the fact that initially, the hearing aids helped him to hear, they also attracted attention that Steven didn't want. Not only did people notice them and talk about them, but they also used the fact that he had hearing aids as a reason to exclude and bully him. Often, and especially in noisy spaces, Steven chose to take the hearing aids out.

Because Steven often relied on his limited hearing, his lack of ability to hear clearly impacted his speech. He had a quiet, higher voice. This too became a reason for others to mistreat him. In fact, he was sometimes punched by older boys and men who wanted to force him to speak more loudly. Ultimately, the mocking of his voice led to selective mutism for Steven.

Steven recalls his mother giving him a notebook to use to write out his thoughts. This opportunity led him to become a prolific writer. He believes that this is where his love of journalism began.

After high school, while he was studying liberal arts at Essex County College, Steven had the opportunity to pursue an internship with Disney in Orlando. Here, he felt accepted and learned to work with and engage with others. Steven stayed connected with Disney for many years. He worked in a Disney store after college and was then promoted to be a host with Radio Disney because his "Storytime with Steven" event in the store had captured the attention of the regional manager. He later had the opportunity to participate with Aladdin on Broadway.

This work led to Steven taking a job as a reporter with a variety of media outlets. It was rare to see a Black male journalist on the red carpet. Unfortunately, this was not a welcoming place for Steven to work.

"There are so many stages of grief when you know that you're going blind."

It was also at this time that Steven began to lose his sight. Initially, he would slip because he didn't realize that there was a flight of stairs in front of him. He also missed cues like someone extending their hand to shake his. People began to believe that he was being rude, but the reality was that his vision was narrowing. In 2019, Steven was diagnosed with usher syndrome.

The next few years were incredibly difficult for Steven. He couldn't imagine what could be ahead for a DeafBlind Black man. After this personal crisis, Steven decided to acknowledge and own his disability. This has opened doors to incredible opportunities.

Steven is a speaker, journalist, and advocate who has taken his message across the world, including to Capitol Hill. Steven is the world's first DeafBlind journalist. He has founded the non-profit organization Spoken Heroes and uses this platform to bridge the gap between the able-bodied and the disability community. In 2024, he was named in the Forbes 40 Under 40 list for his work on behalf of people with disabilities. He works to support those with disabilities to own, but not be inhibited by, their disabilities, so that the non-disabled know us.

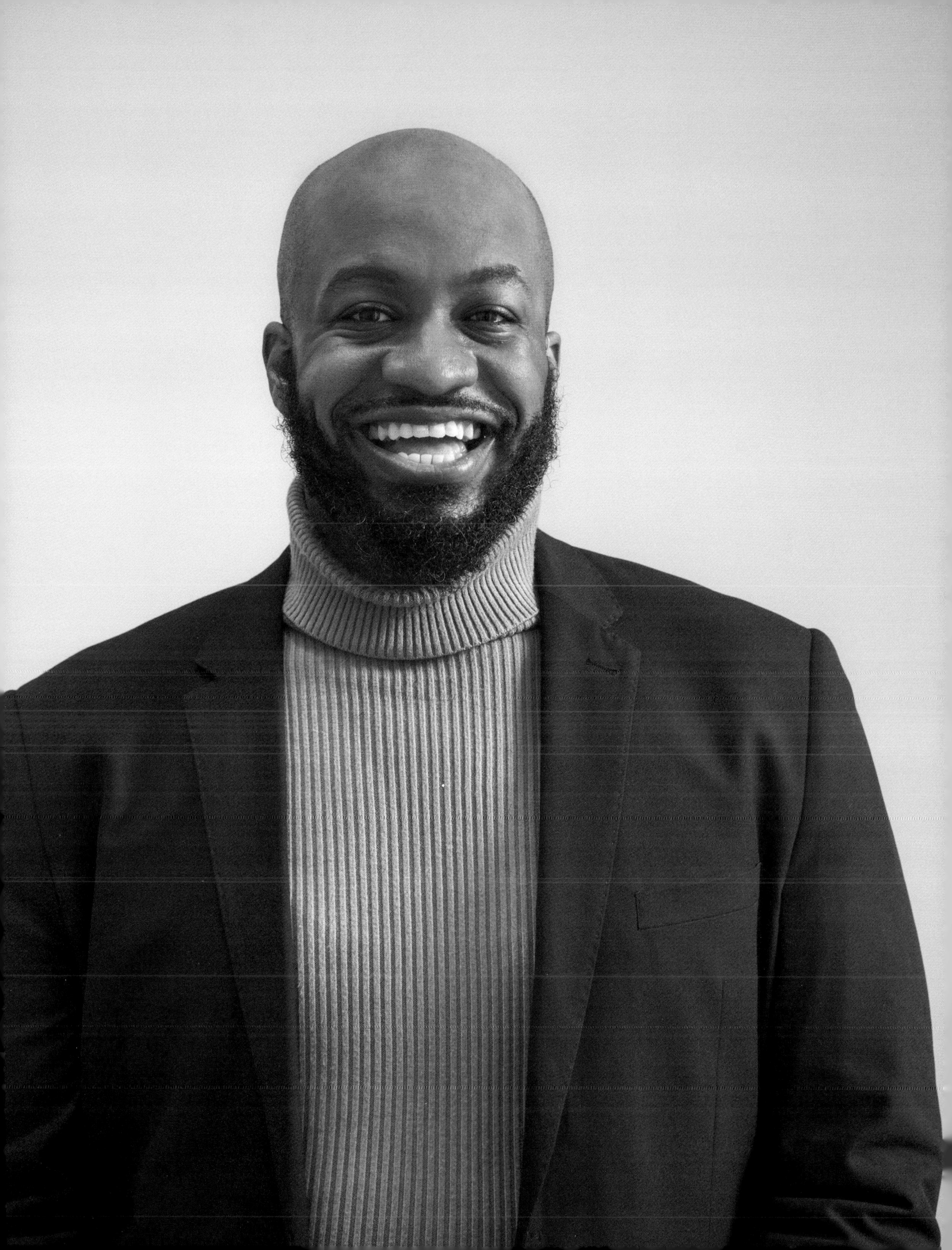

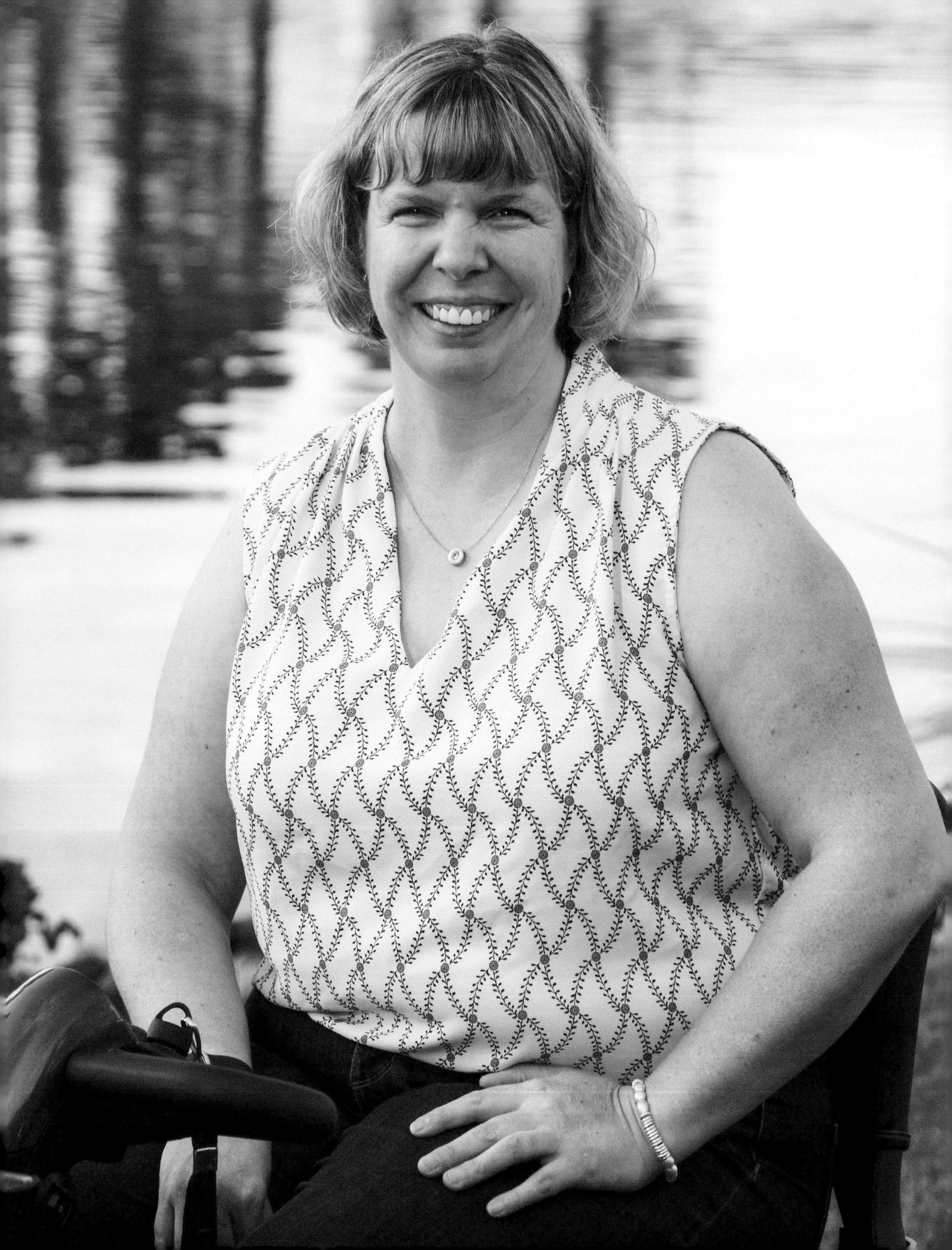

Poem Origin Story

While Darby does identify as a person with a disability, she tries to change the conversation so that she's not seen as "Darby on the Scooter" or as "Scooter Girl." Her scooter doesn't define her—it's how she gets around, but not who she is.

Not only is creating accessible spaces Darby's work, but it is also a commitment that she takes on each day. She cares deeply about reducing the challenges that people with disabilities face in navigating the world, so when she sees a barrier, she points it out to others and addresses changing it any way that she can. Those who have spent a day with her learn to experience the world the way that she and others with disabilities experience it.

It is Darby's hope that the world will progress in a way that leads to accessibility and inclusion and that people with disabilities will be seen as people.

It Takes 30 Minutes More

Will I find a place to park?
With enough space
To unload
My scooter from the car?
Get off the curb
And across the street?
Fit my scooter
Through the door?
Navigate the
Uneven floor?
Access the washroom?

"That can't come in," she said,
Pointing to the scooter.
"It's not a wheelchair...
Why don't you just walk?"

It's talk like this-
Impossible to miss.
In spite of the fact
That I've investigated

The route,
Scoped out
The location,
Looked online at images
Of the restaurant...shop...theatre...venue.
I can't just say,
"Let's go for dinner."
Spontaneity's not
An option.

The cost
Of disability
Is time
Spent.
30 minutes more
To find out
If I can even get in
The door.

Darby Lee Young

Darby learned to walk when she was eight years old; a few years later, she was skiing. Darby was born with cerebral palsy which hasn't kept her from being active for much of her life. Indeed, she was a competitive para-alpine ski racer and worked for the Vancouver Olympics and Paralympics.

While she was able to be independent on the ski slopes, things were harder for Darby at school. For much of her childhood, Darby attended a school that had a second floor but no elevator. As a result, her principal would carry her up and down the stairs. Because children with significant disabilities attended a "special" school designed to meet their needs, there was a misperception in Darby's community that there weren't people with disabilities in their neighborhood. Darby suffered from exclusion and bullying, and thus, she feels strongly that views about people with disabilities need to be changed.

Professionally, Darby began her career by working for building design firms so that she could learn to help builders do more than just meet building code, thus making spaces fully accessible.

In 2015, she started her own company, Level Playing Field, and works to expand what builders recognize as truly inclusive spaces. Level Playing Field focuses on consulting with companies responsible for building new arenas, conference centers, and aquatic centers. Darby also works with universities to provide inclusive and accessible design guidelines. She has had the opportunity to work with transportation organizations to ensure that they design inclusive accessibility plans. Additionally, Darby worked with the Stagecoach Music Festival as a consultant on their accessibility plan.

Efforts to create accessible buildings can be more challenging in Canada, where they have building codes but nothing like the ADA that exists in the United States. Darby works to encourage builders not just to meet but to exceed code so as to build more inclusive spaces.

"People with disabilities need to be seen as people who belong in society. We need to change the mentality around disability, to accept all shapes, sizes, abilities, and forms."

As a result of her efforts to create inclusive accessible buildings and systems, Darby has been recognized as one of Canada's Top 40 Under 40 and included as one of the Top 25 Women of Influence.

Currently, Darby is a certified safeguarding officer via the IOC Safeguarding Program, and as such she participates in the International Olympic Committee Safeguarding Program, which enables her to stay connected to sports and to protect and promote the well-being of athletes.

In spite of the fact that she's a successful athlete, an entrepreneur, and an award-winning business owner, Darby is often seen first as a person with a disability. She is subjected to belittling remarks and comments that she has to endure. She sometimes feels like a "foreign object, begging for [her] life every day."

"I'm trying to make a difference, one day at a time."

Tony Jackson

Tony was born into this world with arthrogryposis, a congenital condition that causes his joints to be stiff and immobile and his muscles to not be fully developed. He was born in Korea, the son of a soldier, and moved a great deal until he left home to go to college. In spite of the fact that he moved a lot, attending three high schools in four years, Tony describes his childhood as a typical one. He did what kids do within his ability to do so.

When he left home to go to Arizona State University (ASU), he faced the same transitions that any other kid going off to college would face, as well as the significant additional transition to a new caregiver who would need to help him with his daily activities and needs. It was difficult for him to trust a stranger for care that he had previously received from his family.

After earning his degree in social work, Tony got a job as an academic counselor for an online university. He didn't love this work, and, encouraged by others who said that he had a great voice, he returned to ASU to earn a degree in broadcast journalism. Here, he found his niche, working at the college radio station and ultimately getting his own show. Over time, he became the production director and later the station manager.

While he bounced around a bit, Tony found himself back in Arizona, where he discovered adaptive sports and, specifically, power soccer. Here, he found a home with Ability360, a center for independent living with an accessible fitness center where he first got work at the reception desk. He also began playing and then coaching power soccer. At this time, he was contacted by a power soccer company in Minnesota that wanted him to be the voice of power soccer by livestreaming the games. A year later, Tony was contacted by a disability nonprofit in New Hampshire for whom he became the power soccer coordinator.

Tony is still involved in all of this work and is doing grant writing and voice-over work. He notes that it is because of his disability that he does what he does. He was raised to be engaged and involved. Broadcasting and power soccer gave him the direction that he needed to pursue the work that he does. He's been able to create a studio that's modified to meet his needs and gives him the freedom to do this work. Tony also travels to tournaments to do live broadcasts of games.

"I've done a lot more than other people with more physical capability than I have, have ever done."

While Tony doesn't consider himself a disability advocate, he says that when people see him and see what he does, this allows them to see the capabilities of all people with disabilities. He's appreciative of the changes that have been made to make the world more accessible. However, he has also experienced personal struggles to maintain his own medical coverage while working, as he was told that he made too much money to still be eligible for coverage. If he lost this coverage, he wouldn't be able to pay for his needed care. The system doesn't consider the needs of people like Tony, and he "would like to see the rules changed." He chooses to use his voice to share his own life experiences.

"People have automatically written a story about me the moment they see me. When they get to know me, the story is rewritten."

Poem Origin Story

Tony distinctly recalls being a beet in his second-grade drama production. He sat onstage in his wheelchair for the whole play until it came time for his classmates to "harvest" him and act as though they were pulling him from the ground. This story came up when I asked Tony if he identified as a person with a disability. For much of his childhood, he was the only wheelchair user at school. He has always identified as a person with a disability and sees how he is different from others.

That said, Tony thinks most about his disability when he comes up against obstacles and barriers. He doesn't wake up in the morning and think, "I'm disabled." However, if he comes to the end of the sidewalk where there isn't a curb cut or needs to use the restroom without an available caregiver, he does feel the impact of inaccessible places and of relying on others as a result of his disability.

Most of the time, and in most ways, Tony thinks of himself as "just a guy," meaning that even though his body isn't typical, he's a typical person in many other ways. When I asked him what it was like living with a disability, Tony struggled to answer the question because he has no baseline for comparison. This is the life he has always lived.

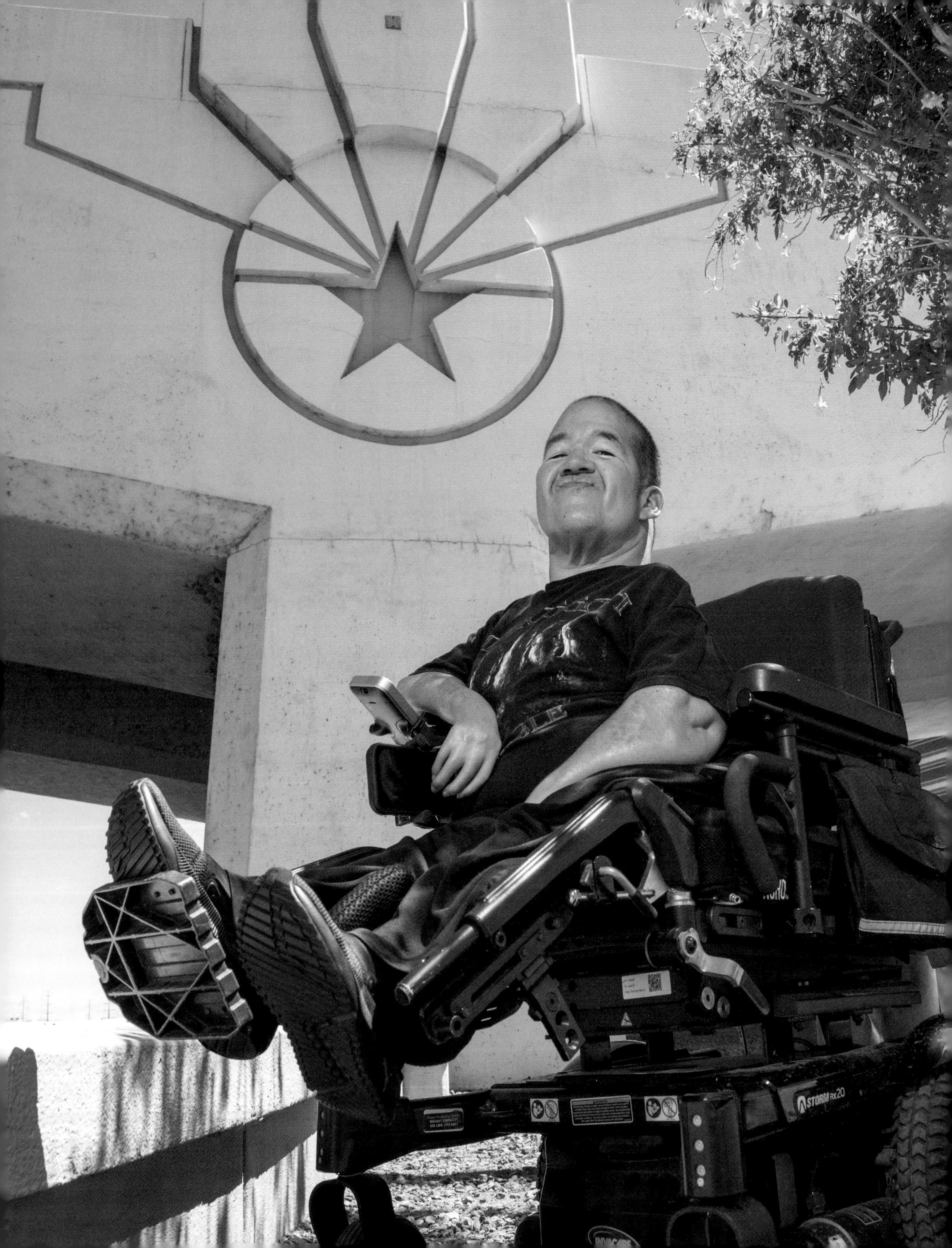
STORM RX20

I Have Always

I have always
Been
In this body,
Been this person.

Have always
Been intelligent,
Able to speak for myself.
Had goals and dreams;
A desire
For romantic relationships.

Have grown
Out
Of anger and frustration
They no longer serve any purpose,
Won't solve any problems.

Instead,
I have accepted
The pact
That society has made with me;
A commitment
A Promise.
That others will
Be there,
Will help me
Each day
To live my full life.

A burden?
No more.
They see the value in me.
Know that
I matter.
Affirm my self- acceptance.

I have always,
Always been.

Poem Origin Story

Melissa used to identify herself as a person with a disability but has stopped doing so because she heard, "You can't do that because you have a disability," too many times. She certainly recognizes that she has cerebral palsy, uses a wheelchair, and has physical challenges, but she balks at the word "can't" and pushes herself to prove that she can.

When Melissa struggles to stay motivated and positive, she has people in her life who talk her through her frustration and support her in moving forward as she faces challenges. She calls these people her rope team, a term taken from climbing with No Barriers. Music is also part of her rope team, as she finds inspiration in listening to songs from artists like Pink and Luke Bryan.

Melissa is often frustrated with people's assumptions about her and wishes that they would talk to her and learn her story.

Rope Team

My rope team
Is ready.

He loops the ropes
Over his shoulders.
She rests her hands
On the back
Of my chair.

My rope team
Is ready.

This chair-
Freedom.

On level ground,
I have the strength
To pull myself
Forward.

On the mountain,
I need.

And my rope team
Is ready.

We all
Have mountains to climb.
Require help
Through life's obstacles.
Help
Turning can't into can.

We can dig deep
When our
Rope team
Is ready.

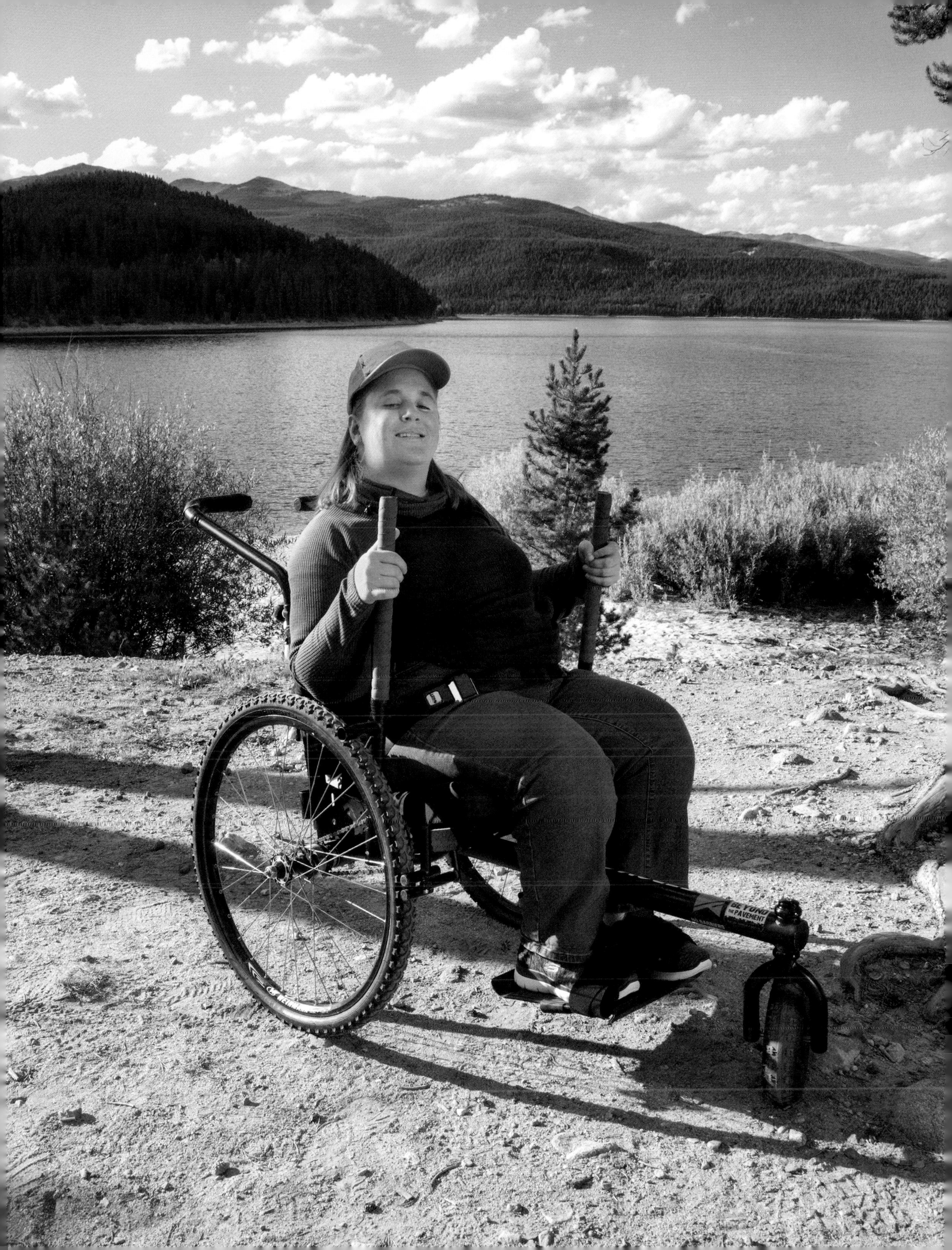

Melissa Simpson

Melissa came into this world three months early, weighing only one pound, fifteen ounces. At the age of two she was diagnosed with spastic diplegia, a form of cerebral palsy that primarily impacts her legs. Melissa has been a wheelchair user since then, though she can use her arms to transfer herself and can do some standing.

Melissa lives in Colorado and attended the local public schools through twelfth grade. While she had an Individualized Education Program (IEP) and had some accommodations, Melissa was an exceptional student and a member of the honor society.

After high school, Melissa attended Colorado Mountain College, ultimately earning an associate's degree in general studies with a focus on patient service coordinating.

It was at her commencement that Melissa made a connection that would change her life. Erik Weihenmayer was the commencement speaker. Erik is a blind athlete who co-founded No Barriers USA, an organization dedicated to helping people face challenges and live purposeful lives. His influence and friendship would ultimately lead Melissa to climb one of the highest peaks in Colorado, one that she had looked at through her window her whole life.

Melissa's climb also led to the making of an award-winning short film, From My Window, that chronicled Melissa's preparation for the climb as well as the climb itself. As a result of this film, Melissa has become an ambassador for No Barriers USA and has participated in showings and speaking engagements related to the film.

As an ambassador, Melissa spreads knowledge about No Barriers and speaks on behalf of what No Barriers does for at-risk youth, people with mental and physical disabilities, veterans, and caregivers. She also teaches people about the No Barriers lifestyle and speaks about and shares the organization's mission in order to get more people involved.

Most recently, Melissa has been working as a volunteer at Howard Head Sports Medicine in Vail, Colorado. Here, she assists with a variety of tasks and talks to patients to make sure that

"I've always wanted to climb these mountains and to be outside."

they have what they need. She also has taken on the role of coordinating and recruiting volunteers and reporting on volunteer-related items to the board. The staff and patients make Melissa feel appreciated and this work gives her purpose.

Melissa also works with a local committee to get the Lake County swimming pool reopened and up to ADA code so that people with disabilities will be able to access it.

Melissa is an avid skier and has participated in hiking, rock climbing, paddleboarding, and archery. She loves to be outside!

"Gotta dream big dreams and work hard to tackle your goals."

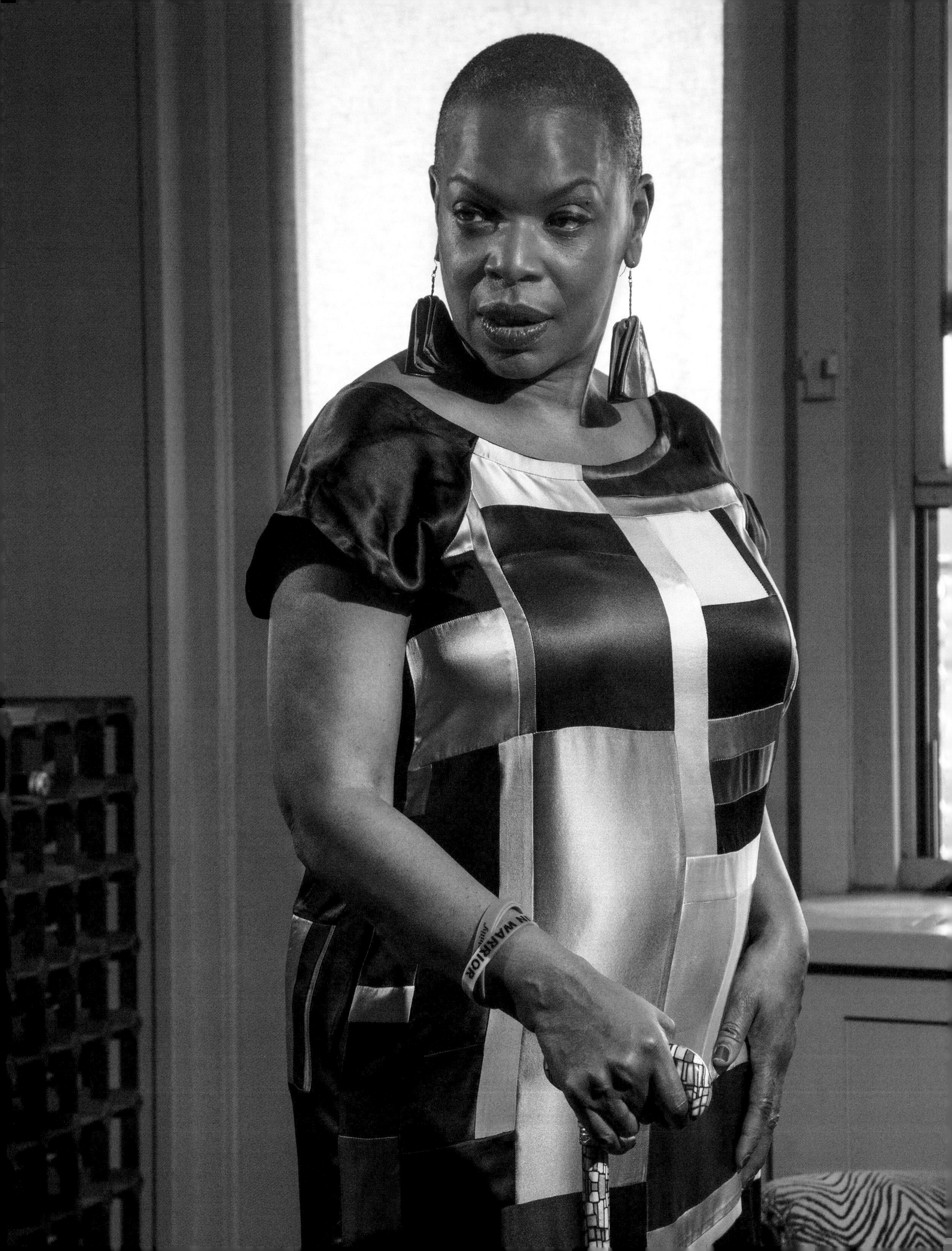
WARRIOR

Zazel O'Garra

Zazel's family is from the small Caribbean island of Montserrat. She credits her lively energy and vibrant family life to this Caribbean ancestry and culture. Zazel grew up in Queens, New York, and started dancing when she was eight years old. As a child, she recalls studying at Ruth Williams Dance Studio and Bernice Johnson Dance Center and performing at Lincoln Center and Carnegie Hall.

Zazel attended the High School of Performing Arts and then majored in dance at the University of Michigan. After graduating, Zazel went back to New York and began to audition for dance companies and musical theatre. Between jobs, she worked as a hostess at the Parker Meridian Hotel. It was here that she was approached by the cover editor of Essence Magazine who invited her to be a cover model for the magazine. This led to other opportunities in modeling, dancing, acting, commercials, and musical theatre, as well as representation by CESD talent agency and Wilhelmina Models.

When Zazel reached her mid thirties, the roles that she was getting changed. Suddenly, she was the mom in the parts that she played and the commercials that she did. It was also at this time that she started getting symptoms of what ultimately was a brain tumor. She started to experience extreme fatigue, arm tremors, headaches, and later seizures. After being dismissed by doctors who said that nothing was wrong with her, Zazel finally was given an MRI and her meningioma (a four centimeter benign brain tumor) was discovered.

> *"Though it was a traumatic diagnosis, I felt at ease that they had discovered what was wrong."*

She was told that she needed to have the tumor removed, and in doing so risked paralysis, cognitive deficit, and speech impairment. Certainly, this was difficult news for a dancer to hear.

Following the surgery, Zazel did experience paralysis on her right side. Through extensive physical, occupational, and speech therapy, she regained significant mobility and is able to move most of her body. While her right foot and leg remain partially paralyzed, requiring the use of a brace and cane, she continues to dance with determination and grace.

In addition to earning a master's degree in social work, Zazel joined many disability organizations and focused her energy on being an advocate for people with disabilities. She also started ZCO/Dance Project, a physically integrated dance company.

ZCO/Dance Project approaches dance as healing, and works to integrate and include individuals with disabilities, giving them a platform for expression and the opportunity to build their skills and confidence. Zazel hopes that when people see her dancers, they see people's humanity and capacity.

The first time that Zazel spoke and then performed after her surgery, she felt a sense of rebirth and resurrection. Today, she dances mostly in a chair but puts all of her grace and energy into her upper body, so that she can be as expressive and passionate as possible. Zazel's mantra is "Turning setbacks into comebacks!"

"In spite of the fact that I've had tremendous notoriety and acclaim, because I'm disabled, I am still not looked at as a success."

Poem Origin Story

Full steam ahead is how Zazel describes her approach to life. In spite of, or maybe because of, her challenges with disability, she feels compelled and committed to serving others in the disability community. Zazel spends her time advocating for others and helping them to navigate the health care and public support systems.

While she does view herself as a person with a disability, she says that often those around her do not see her as such. She presents herself as an active person, a dancer, a model, and a hard worker who likes to choose fancy clothes. Both this outward appearance, and the strong attitude with which she carries herself enable her to downplay the pain that she is in and the struggles that she experiences.

She shared that the journey continues—she's come to terms with what's happening in her body and even though it's not easy, she shows up each day. Zazel finds grace in her ability to laugh deeply and to find humor even in the darkest of places.

Still A Warrior

The land
I come from-
Colonized by those
Not indigenous.
A foreign
Intrusion
That changed us.
An Ivory wall
Built in
Black sand.[1]

My body,
Like this ancestral home,
Is host
To that which
Doesn't belong,
Doesn't serve us.

Tremendous peaks
And deep valleys
Of my land,
And the landscape
Of my body.
Both are changed
Over time.

My wall
Of strength
Sensitivity,
Radiance-
Visible
Through the lens
As I transform.

And thus,
In spite
Of the pain
And the fear.
I laugh.

[1] Howard Fergus This Land is Mine

Reverend Chris Wylie (DJ Pastor Rock)

After being born premature and weighing three pounds, Chris was taken home from the hospital by a family that would ultimately adopt him. He later learned that, at the time of his birth, his biological mother was told that he might not live and that if he did, he would have no quality of life, so she ought to leave him there.

When he was young, Chris watched his sister learn to stand and walk, and he copied her. He didn't become a wheelchair user until later in his life. Throughout his childhood, Chris played sports and participated in SABAH, the Skating Association for the Blind and Handicapped in Buffalo, New York, where Chris grew up. Because he was such an active athlete with this organization, Chris appeared in TV and newspaper stories and advertisements about the association.

Chris worked for many years in consumer business and financial services, after earning his college degree in business. While doing this work, he met Bernice, a friend that he describes as "peaceful," saying that her friendship made him want to pursue working for justice.

"I just want to help people. If you want someone to be there in it with you, I'm your person."

At the same time, while Chris was experiencing a back injury that required surgery, and feeling his body breaking down, he felt a calling to go to seminary. Chris pursued this calling and was ordained as a United Methodist Church minister. For the next fifteen years, Chris was the pastor at several small, rural churches outside of Buffalo, New York.

In his work as a pastor, Chris was told that he had a way of "breaking things down so that people could understand." Because of his disability, and his Queer identity, Chris knows what it feels like to be on the outside. In his ministry, he has made deliberate efforts to make sure that members of his congregation don't feel this way. He is on, he says, a "never ending quest for peace.

Ten years ago, Chris stepped away from his ministry because his cerebral palsy was impacting his body more, requiring that he use his wheelchair full time; even his own churches weren't fully accessible. While Chris had incorporated music into his pastoral work, when he stepped away, he began to more directly pursue his music.

Chris writes, records, and performs his music which he calls "angsty Gen X rock." He also continues to focus his music on themes related to justice and peace. While he does play guitar and drums, Chris is mostly a singer, songwriter, and lyricist. He is also a member of the punk band Moshcats.

> *"I can preach and write songs that help people to be seen because I know what it's like to be on the outside."*

In addition to writing and recording music, Chris works with RAMPD (Recording Artists and Music Professionals with Disabilities) and is the treasurer for the organization. Chris's first album, Rolling Nation, was well received and enabled him to form a nonprofit organization that raises money to provide grants for those needing wheelchair accessible vans. In 2023, Chris was named as an Honoree on the D 30 Disability Impact List. He also was awarded a 2024 Wavy award for historically excluded and marginalized musicians.

Chris says that he has never met a microphone that he didn't like.

Poem Origin Story

When we begin our conversation, Chris recognizes that his disability is and has always been visible, so he's claimed it as part of his identity. Indeed, there was no way that he could hide it, so he openly acknowledges it. That said, he's also adamant that his disability is only a part of his much larger identity.

Chris sees himself as a spouse, a parent, a musician, a pastor, a friend, a neighbor, and more. He is all of these things in a body that's disabled. His life, he says, is "multifaceted, and inherently worthwhile."

While he wants people to see all of these parts of his identity, Chris also wants people to see his disability. It's part of him and he feels that it needs to be included. He doesn't want people to "look past it," as it is part of what makes him who he is.

Chris says that he doesn't think about his body much more than a non disabled person thinks about their body. He's more aware of his disability when people make infantilizing remarks or question the value of his life.

Building relationships between disabled and non disabled people is the way to create connection and understanding, Chris believes. If people know each other in ways that aren't limited to the condition of the bodies that they inhabit, they will see the depth of people and be able to build relationships.

"Barriers," Chris says, "are broken down by building such relationships."

Not to be Overcome

My disabled body-
A part of me.
It has made
Me who I am.

It carries me
Each day,

My eyes, see the sun.
Ears, hear the birds.
Cheeks, feel the breeze.
Lips receive my child's sweet kiss.
My hands, hold my wife's hands.
Songs and sermons-
I give voice to.

This disability-
Not something that I can,
Want,
Need,
To overcome.

Instead, I adjust the framing
And embrace.
My body, my self
This rich life
That I'm living.

Insistent,
I am.
And I am
Centered
In my own narrative.

Spouse, father, friend, neighbor, pastor,
songwriter, singer...and more

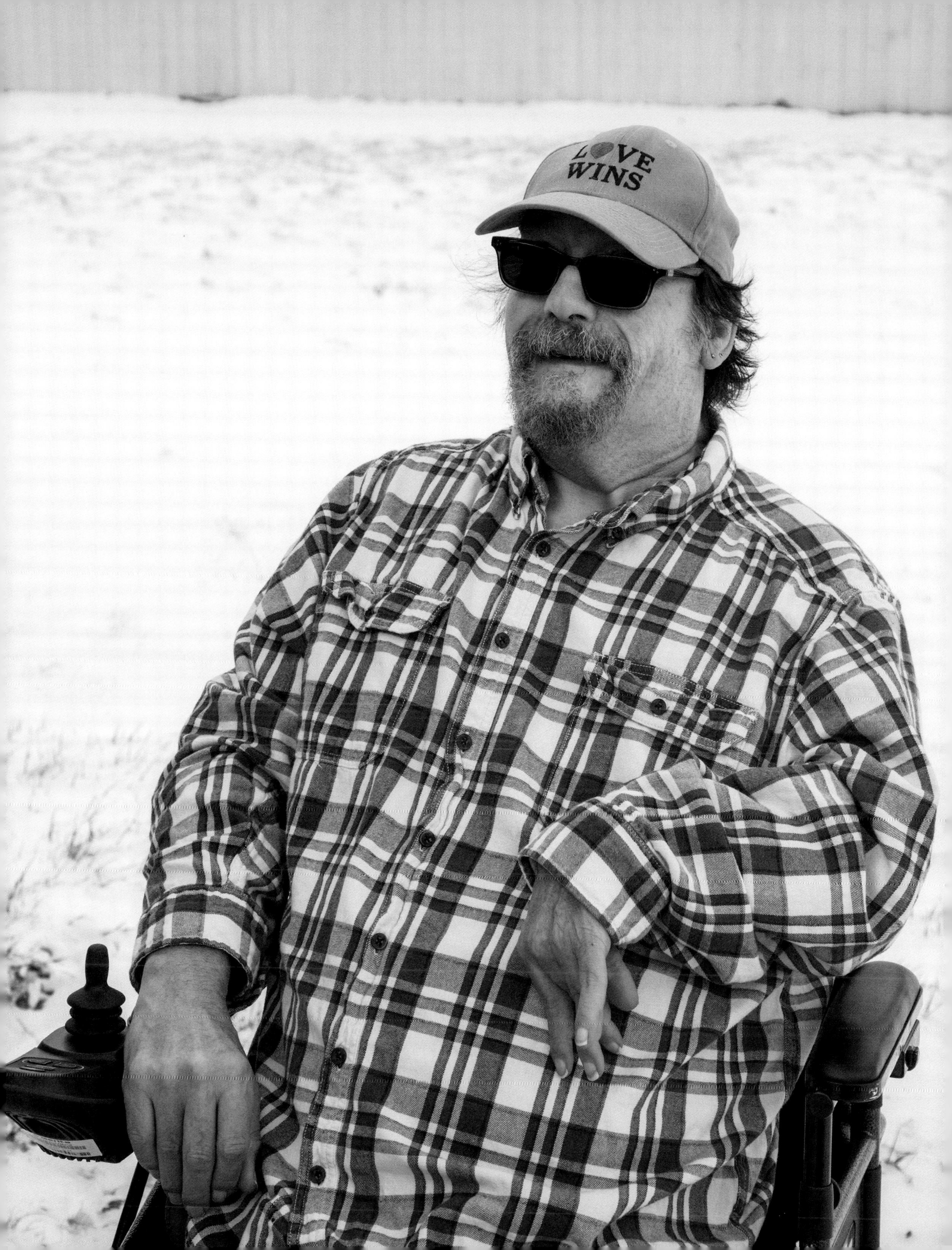
LOVE
WINS

Penn Street

At first, it didn't register to Penn why the mirrors had been taken down in her hospital room. When she was nine, she was bitten by a rattlesnake and, as a result of the antivenom and medications that she was given, she contracted Stevens Johnson syndrome (SJS), a life threatening condition that impacts soft tissue, including the face and the eyes. Her appearance was so changed that when she did see herself, she believed that she was seeing a monster and didn't recognize her own face. Her doctors and family had been trying to spare her this experience. Since then, she has had the opportunity to meet others with facial differences, which has led to her own healing.

Penn had been a healthy, active kid who prided herself on being a tomboy and, as she was the ninth of ten children, she was accustomed to keeping up with her eight older siblings and spending time with her younger sister. Suddenly, instead of being seen this way, she was seen as sick and fragile by her family and friends, as well as by strangers. Trying to integrate back into her life was a challenge. Often, she was discouraged from going outside and from being too active, as the SJS also affected her heart and lungs. For Penn, it also led to vision loss.

She first began to come back to herself when she worked with a teacher who taught her to navigate the world as a blind person. Penn was told, "You can do more than they're letting you do," and was encouraged to gain the confidence to do more, including horseback riding and going away to camp where she met other blind children.

As a child, Penn was very aware that she benefited from special teachers and community members who impacted her life in a positive way, ensuring that she had what she needed to be as independent as possible. Her experiences with these "superheroes" made it clear to Penn that she wanted her life's work to be this kind of work on behalf of others with disabilities.

"On a cellular level, I was not the same kid. I was not treated the same way... not looked at the same way, in spite of the fact that I felt the same."

"It's always a battle, even to this day, with people saying that you shouldn't be doing that because... Instead, it's important to surround yourself with people who say yes."

Penn has spent her professional life working as a special education teacher, as well as working for nonprofit organizations dedicated to serving people with disabilities. Her roles have ranged from ADA coordinator to outreach and development manager. When she worked for No Barriers, a nonprofit organization that provides services for people with disabilities in gaining the skills and confidence necessary to tackle challenges, Penn was encouraged and inspired to up her game, even rafting the entire Grand Canyon.

When she was working at a school for students with disabilities, a photographer came to take pictures of the students who were reluctant to have their photos taken. Penn allowed him to take hers so that the others would be more willing to have their own pictures taken. She recalls the feeling of being treated like she was beautiful. This photographer, Moses, became her husband. He also helped her to venture back outdoors in a way that she hadn't for a long time. Together, they have shared many years of skiing, camping, and hiking.

Three and a half years ago, Penn was encouraged to do a podcast, and The Blind Chick was born. She has used this platform to bring in "ordinary" people who share their extraordinary stories. In this way, Penn continues to advocate for people with disabilities by helping them to be heard.

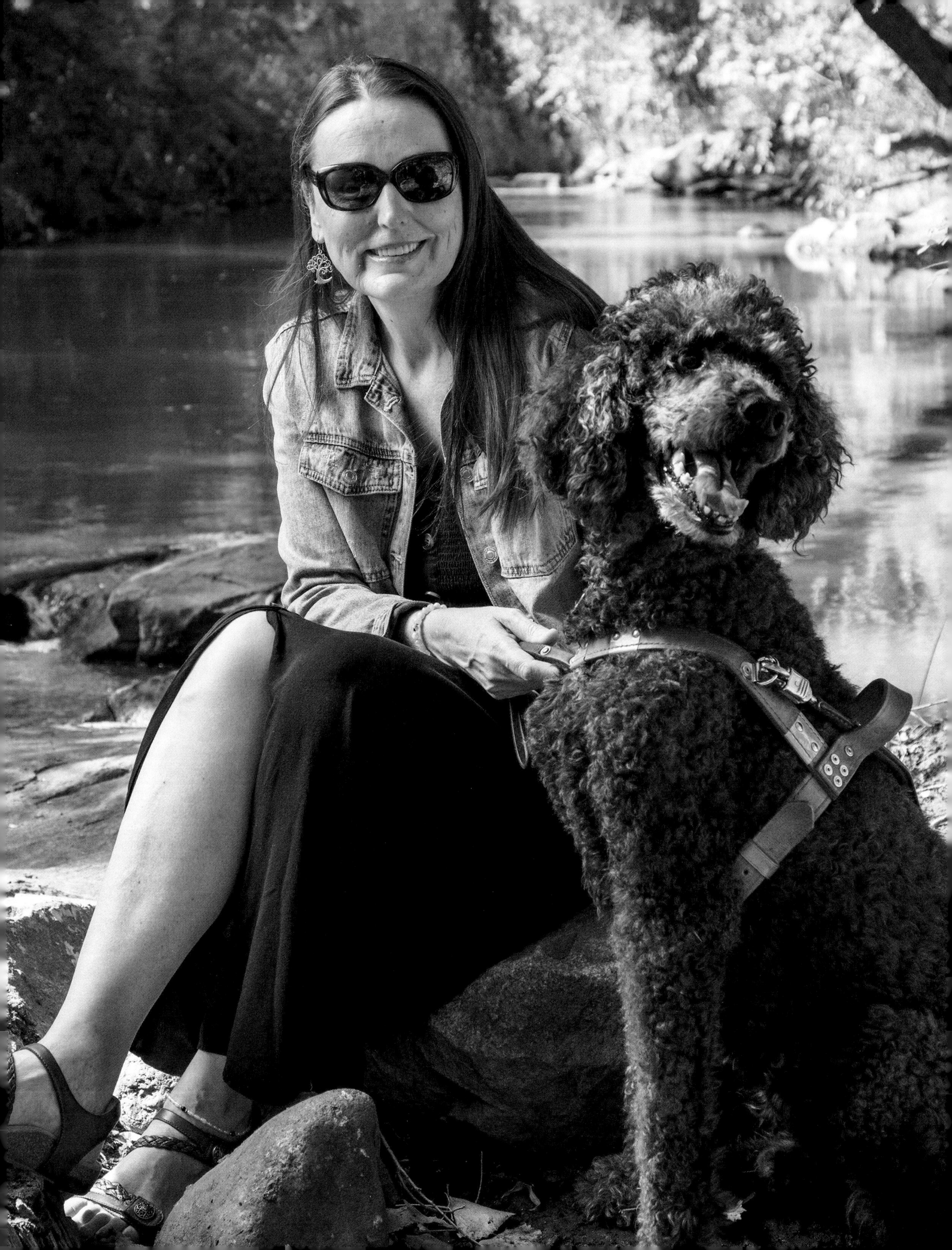

Poem Origin Story

When Penn was a child, she didn't think of herself as a person with a disability. She just had vision loss and still felt that she could do most things, so it didn't feel to her like she was disabled. She associated disability with age, and since she was young, the term didn't apply to her. It wasn't until she was in college and qualified for the disabled skiing program that, upon meeting other people with vision loss who identified as disabled, Penn began to feel like part of this community.

At home, Penn doesn't feel limited, as she is able to control her environment. Being spontaneous, though, is hard. She can't just grab her keys and go. Instead, even the smallest trips away from home require planning and organizing. She has to have a plan, and a backup plan, anytime that she ventures out. This, she notes, is the most exhausting part of living with a disability.

She lives with and navigates constant assessments from other people: people who send her information about new treatments for her vision, those who make comments about how lucky she is to be taken care of, people who think that she's braver than she is, and even people who think that she's cheating at games and must be able to see because she's so good!

Penn has been told throughout her life that she would only live to be nine...fifteen...twenty five.... Having surpassed all of these deadlines, she doesn't feel afraid anymore and simply wants to help others with disabilities and to be out in the sunshine as much as she can be.

The Last Time

The last hike
I took
May be
The last hike
I'll take.

The last time
I went skiing,
Was that
The last time
That I'll go skiing?

Will I
Be okay
Sitting
On the shore
Instead
Of in a kayak
Or on a paddleboard?

If I had seen it
As such,
Would I have held on
To each moment
Of joy,
Or been
Overcome with sadness?

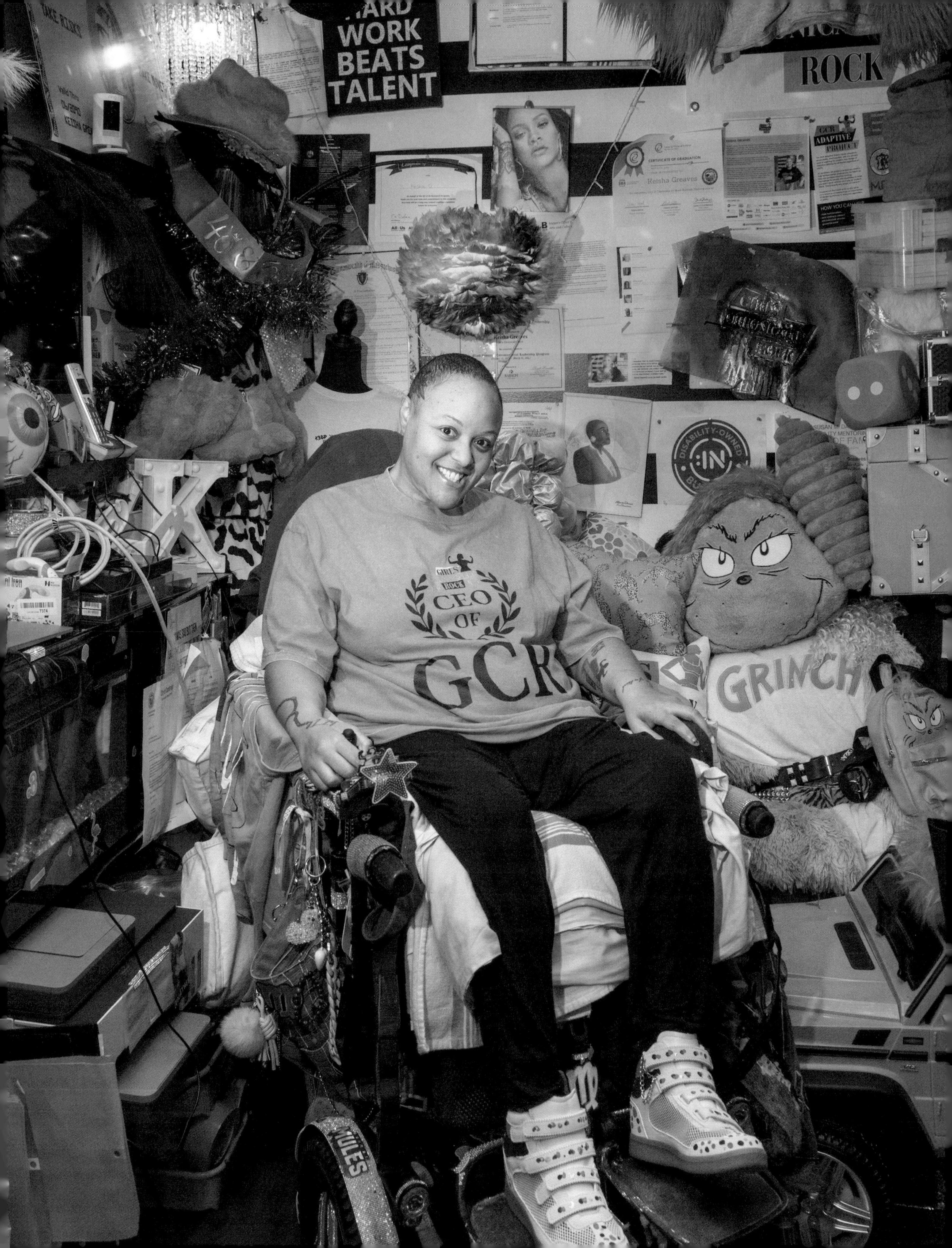
HARD WORK BEATS TALENT
ROCK
TAKE RISKS!
CERTIFICATE OF GRADUATION
Keisha Greaves
GCR ADAPTIVE PROJECT
DISABILITY-OWNED
GIRLS ROCK
CEO OF GCR
GRINCH
MILES

Keisha Greaves

Keisha always knew that she'd have a career in fashion, she just had no idea that she would use her fashion and business degrees to create adaptive fashion lines. Keisha was born and raised in Cambridge, Massachusetts, and, in spite of having significant breathing problems when she was born, she had a fairly typical childhood filled with playing outside and on the softball field.

While Keisha had experienced some early signs of what was finally diagnosed as muscular dystrophy, she brushed those off as just symptoms of being tired or needing to lose weight. A few times when she was young, she would experience a feeling that her leg was going to give out, or she would have a problem of her arm not extending fully. These passed, so she assumed that she was fine. It was not until 2010 when her leg gave out, causing her to fall, and to need help getting up, that Keisha saw a neurologist and was diagnosed with muscular dystrophy.

"For me, losing that control is still a challenge each and every day."

Initially, Keisha was skeptical about this diagnosis. It just didn't seem that she could really have this disease. There is no cure, no treatment, and the disease is progressive. While she did start treatments and physical therapy, she also tried to make her illness go away. She often chose to stay home and made excuses for her cane when she did go out: "Oh, I sprained my ankle...I was in a car accident..." She told people everything but the truth.

It was only when she began to blog about her experiences that Keisha found that she could come to accept her diagnosis and move forward in her life. It took her time to acknowledge her illness, but as she did so, she found herself inspired to create her own adaptive clothing line, Girls Chronically Rock. In 2023 she was able to show her line in both the New York and the Miami fashion weeks.

"Designing and producing clothes that allow people to dress independently allows for them to be confident."

In addition to creating her own adaptive clothing line, Keisha has become a disability rights advocate. She serves on several boards, including the Commission for People with Disabilities in Cambridge, Massachusetts. She's working to create guidelines that will require that more housing for people with disabilities be developed.

Keisha has also started the GCR (Girls Chronically Rock) Adaptive Project, a nonprofit organization that works with fashion design students to teach them about adaptive fashion and to guide them as they create their own adaptive clothes.

Her muscular dystrophy has progressed, and Keisha now uses a wheelchair and needs daily care. "Some days," she says, "I don't know what the body's going to feel like. I have to follow the rules of MD." Despite this uncertainty, Keisha continues to create new adaptive designs and to advocate for people with disabilities. She appreciates the community that she's become a part of, as she feels like people with disabilities share a common understanding of each other's challenges.

Poem Origin Story

At the beginning of our conversation, Keisha shares that because she was diagnosed with muscular dystrophy later in life, identifying herself as a person with a disability was a process. Initially, she sometimes told people that she'd been in a car accident, instead of disclosing her diagnosis. Now, she's able to say, "This is who I am," and to open people's eyes to what a person with a disability has to deal with.

While Keisha is a person who likes to be in control, she has accepted that she can't control her disease, recognizing that each day brings a different challenge. Perhaps her impatience spurs her on, as she is active and engaged with the world around her. She is deeply committed to fashion and to her own adaptive fashion line. Keisha has also embraced being a disability advocate and regularly speaks and advocates for inclusion.

Keisha expressed that prior to her diagnosis, she was an independent person, and now as she has to rely on caregivers, she can't be independent in the same way. This has been one of her greatest challenges. The more that the world is accessible, the more that she can do for herself, and thus she uses her voice to advocate.

You Have No Idea

I am not
One
To stay home,
In bed.

Most of us are not.

We have rich lives
Businesses,
Friends,
Partners,
In spite of the daily challenges
Our diseases,
And the world,
Have brought upon us.

When I
Show up...
You have no idea
How much I have done
To arrive.

You have no idea.
Everything has to be planned-
I have to rely on others.

There's no way to tell my disease,
"Go away.
Today is not for you."

My patience,
A work in progress.
It's human to feel frustration
And anger
As we struggle
To do
What once we could,
And can no longer..

And yet,
Daily,
We smile,
Laughing at what brings us joy.
Proud, successful, enthusiastic
Because, and in spite of our struggles.
Our purpose,
Simply,
To be ourselves.
To live deeply.

You have no idea.
So we tell you.
Please
Listen.

Acknowledgements

I would not have been able to do this without the love and faith of my husband, Kevin. Thank you for believing in me and in this project, and for the time that you gave me to invest in this and for your willingness to take the lion's share of the work at home. I am so very grateful!

I am also so appreciative of each person who gave me their time and trust and shared their stories with me. This book is what it is because the people whose stories I've told are unique and amazing and they were willing to be vulnerable and raw in what they shared with me. I have made thirty wonderful friends and have found such a lively, rich community of people who both affirm and challenge me.

I'm grateful to Natalie Brescia, who agreed to be the project photographer and to travel the country taking portraits. She's an amazingly talented and lovely human being who has been so open and willing to connect with the people whose portraits she's taken. I'm so proud of who she is and of her talent and commitment to exceptional work.

Dr. Donna Walton agreed to take on the foreword for this book, and I am so appreciative of her perspective, wisdom, and ability to communicate so eloquently. Her voice and her vision come through in what she writes and in her belief in this project. I am humbled by her commitment to creating inclusive, uplifting spaces for women of color with disabilities.

Mary Motley Kalergis has developed some of the most beautiful books, combining her portraits with interviews and stories of people's lives, identities, and communities. I am so appreciative of her willingness to talk with me as I've created this book. Her help and encouragement draw a line between me and my father, Gary Chassman, whose company, Verve Editions, helped her to develop some of her books.

My friend, unofficial editor, and sounding board, Monica Gillespie was always willing to encourage me and to look over what I've written. Thank you, Pooh.

I also want to give a shout out to The Good Listening Project (TGLP). If it weren't for my experience in their listener poet cohort, this book would not be as rich as it is. I'm particularly appreciative of Jenny and Ravenna's support! You can find TGLP here: https://www.goodlistening.org/

I'm so excited to have these words and images out there in the world. Thank you all for your help, guidance and faith in me and this project!

Appendix

Contact Information for Author:

Website: https://jenniferchassmanbrowne.com/
Website: https://newground.us/index.html
Facebook: https://www.facebook.com/jennifer.chassman
Facebook: https://www.facebook.com/JenniferChassmanBrowneAuthor/
LinkedIn: https://www.linkedin.com/in/jennifer-chassman-browne-97768b24a/?skipRedirect=true
Email: jachassman@gmail.com

Contact Information for People Profiled:

Shameka Andrews

Instagram: https://www.instagram.com/disabilityempowered/
YouTube: https://www.youtube.com/@shamekaandrews
Facebook: https://www.facebook.com/ShamekaLAndrews/
LinkedIn: https://www.linkedin.com/in/shameka-andrews-4a010430/recent-activity/all/

Charlie Carr

Website: CharlieCarr.com
Oral History: https://digicoll.lib.berkeley.edu/record/221950?ln=en&v=pdf

Eve Clark

Website: www.disableddivatravels.com
Instagram: https://www.instagram.com/disabled.diva.travels/ or @disabled.diva.travels
Email: eve@disableddivatravelos.com

Arielle Dance

Website: www.drarielledance.com
Instagram: @DrDanceWrites

Hope Demetriades

Website: http://hopedemetriades.com/

Nicole Demos
Instagram: https://www.instagram.com/nixdemos/
Facebook: https://www.facebook.com/nicole.demos.58
LinkedIn: https://www.linkedin.com/in/nicole-levina-maria-demos-she-her-hers-disabled-1a404131/
https://www.tieonline.com/newsletters/73/1/newsletter_2025_01_29
https://womenemerging.org/women-leading-with-disability-empathy-and-strength-a-poem-from-the-women-emerging-expedition/

Cassie Enea
Website: https://commongroundsociety.org/

Jennifer Gasner
Website: https://jennifergasner.com/
Instagram: https://www.instagram.com/jennygwriter/
Facebook: https://www.facebook.com/AuthorJenniferGasner/
LinkedIn: https://www.linkedin.com/in/jennifer-gasner-4b1aaa50/
Amazon: https://www.amazon.com/My-Unexpected-Life-Finding-Diagnosis/dp/B0CCCPG1ZJ/ref=tmm_pap_swatch_0?_encoding=UTF8&qid=1699749170&sr=8-1
Goodreads: https://www.goodreads.com/book/show/61850778-my-unexpected-life
Bookbub: https://www.bookbub.com/authors/jennifer-gasner

Keisha Greaves
Website: www.girlschronicallyrock.com
Instagram: @girlschronicallyrock
YouTube: Girls Chronically Rock
Facebook: Girls Chronically Rock
Twitter/X: @girlschronicrock
LinkedIn: Keisha Greaves
Shop: Girls Chronically Rock Store
Email: kgreaves@girlschronicallyrock.com Phone: 617-888-0561

Trevor Hahn
Instagram: http://www.instagram.com/Trevor_Hahns_Art_Through_Touch

Jane Hash
Instagram: https://www.instagram.com/janehashcnhp/
YouTube: https://www.youtube.com/@JaneHashCNHP
Facebook: https://www.facebook.com/OIamHealthy
Twitter/X: https://x.com/JaneHashCNHP
Bluesky: https://bsky.app/profile/janehash.bsky.social

Maxwell Ivey
Website: www.theblindblogger.net
Facebook: www.facebook.com/maxwellivey
LinkedIn: www.linkedin.com/in/maxwellivey
Instagram: www.instagram.com/TheBlindBlogger
YouTube: www.youtube.com/maxwellivey

Tony Jackson
Website: https://tonyjacksonvo.com
Instagram, YouTube, Facebook, LinkedIn: @TonyJacksonVO

Keith Jones
Website: www.DaSoulToucha.com
Instagram, Twitter/X, Threads, TikTok, Snapchat: @dasoultoucha

Chelsea Lesner-Buxton
Email: Clesnerbuxton@gmail.com

Jacob Lesner-Buxton
Facebook: https://www.facebook.com/jacob.lesnerbuxton/
Email: jakeoaktown@gmail.com

Kate Levinstein
Email: katewrenhealing@gmail.com.

Steven McCoy
Website: https://spokenheroes.org/
Instagram: @stevenmccoy
YouTube: https://youtube.com/@spokenent?si=n756YmKCl4jY-yeg and https://youtube.com/@spokenheroes?si=8lGttWeZpM7mTB6w
https://www.instagram.com/spokenheroes?igsh=bGk1dDlzOXczaGw0&utm_source−qr
Facebook: https://www.facebook.com/share/1A1ePNSBbz/?mibextid=wwXIfr and
https://www.facebook.com/share/1A4gbH7Fe1/?mibextid=wwXIfr
Twitter/X: https://x.com/stevenmccoyb?s=21&t=s-plAeDDVcExV6afjZ7okA and
https://x.com/spokenheroes?s=21&t=s-plAeDDVcExV6afjZ7okA
Linktree: https://linktr.ee/Stevenmccoyb
Donate: https://www.paypal.com/ncp/payment/DJE3P2MCK9MTG
Email: steven@spokenent.com and info@spokenheroes.org

Nico Meyering
Email: meyeringn@gmail.com
LinkedIn: https://www.linkedin.com/in/nicolasmeyering/

Amanda Murray
Instagram: https://www.instagram.com/amandafilm_89/

Zazel O'Garra
Website: https://www.zcodanceproject.com
Website: https://www.zcogarra.com
LinkedIn: https://www.linkedin.com/in/zazel-chavah-o-garra-msw-95b90849
Facebook: /zcodanceproject.com
Instagram: https://www.instagram.com/zco.danceproject
Instagram: https://www.instagram.com/zazelchavah
Twitter/X: twitter.com/zcodanceproject
Email: zcodanceproject1@gmail.com

Matthew Shapiro
Website: https://www.6wheelsconsulting.com
LinkedIn: https://www.linkedin.com/company/6-wheels-consulting-llc/?viewAsMember=true
Website: https://www.matthewshapirospeaking.com/host-matthew
Linktree: https://linktr.ee/matthewshapiro22
X: https://x.com/6WConsulting
Facebook: https://www.facebook.com/6WheelsConsultingLLC
Instagram: https://www.instagram.com/6wheelsconsulting/
TikTok: https://www.tiktok.com/@matthew_6.wheels?lang=en
YouTube: https://www.youtube.com/channel/UC4WSA3Q0lDny_d4cYnKzxYw?

Melissa Simpson
Vimeo: https://vimeo.com/518404753/e7573d794b

Puneet Singh Singhal
LinkedIn: https://www.linkedin.com/in/puneet-singhal/
Linktree: https://linktr.ee/GreenDisability

Sarah Thompson
Website: https://www.drsaratthompson.org/

Dominick Trevethan
Website: https://www.thedisabilitymyth.com/
Instagram: @domdman https://www.instagram.com/domdman?igsh=ZnRyb2ZxeTdkcTg3&utm_source=qr
Email: dom24dt@gmail.com
Podcast: https://open.spotify.com/show/0d7xyhiVocFTvbtYUy5DYB?si=6bMsRkwcQtW7BEiJai1xDA

Saran Tugsjargal
Edsource:https://edsource.org/2025/student-advocacy-california-disability-special-education/741426
Website: https://mhanational.org/youth-leadership/2025-youth-policy-accelerator/
LinkedIn: https://www.linkedin.com/in/saran-tugsjargal/
Instagram: https://www.instagram.com/moonperfect/

Chris Wylie (DJ Pastor Rock)
Email: djpastorrock@gmail.com

Darby Lee Young
Linkedin:www.linkedin.com/in/darby-lee-young
https://www.linkedin.com/company/level-playing-field-inc-/

How to be an Ally; Next Steps to Take

1. Keep learning! The stories that you've read here are just a few of the disability experiences that people have. Continue to educate yourself, to read about people with disabilities, and to take advantage of disability, and disability-related events to build your understanding of and connections to people with disabilities.

2. Leverage your privilege and influence to promote inclusion. Speak up when you have concerns about access. If you're planning an event, include questions about access needs in the registration. Speak to people with disabilities, not for them or around them. Offer assistance, but accept that help may not be needed or wanted. Actively include people with disabilities.

3. Participate in, and encourage your organization to offer disability culture and etiquette training sessions-led by people with disabilities.

4. Normalize accessibility and encourage your organization to build accessible spaces. Provide a variety of options (seating, listening, captions, alt text, ASL interpreters, agendas in advance... etc.) to ensure that all people have access and feel that they belong.

5. Avoid ableist language (e.g., "crippled," "lame," "special needs") and focus on preferred terminology. If you're not sure what someone prefers, ask them.

6. Respect invisible disabilities: Understand that not all disabilities are visible; never assume someone is not disabled because they do not "look" like it.

7. Call out ableism: Challenge discriminatory, patronizing, or stereotypical language and behaviors.

8. Advocate for disability rights. Seek out organizations like; Disability Rights Education and Defense Fund (DREDF), American Association of People with Disabilities (AAPD), The ARC, The National Disability Rights Network (NDRN), American Disabled for Attendant Programs Today (ADAPT), National Council on Disability, National Council on Independent Living, World Institute on Disability, RespectAbility.org, as well as local organizations that support people with disabilities. All are welcome to join!

Contributors

Natalie Brescia

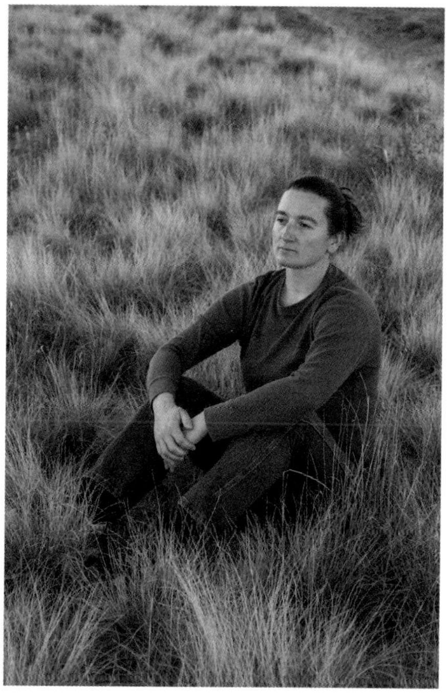

Natalie Brescia (b. 1994) is an artist based in the United States, working across photography, handmade books, sculpture, and installation. Growing up on the Central Coast of California, she draws inspiration from the natural landscapes which she spent her childhood exploring. Whether hiking in the mountains, cactus peeping in the desert, or camping by the ocean, the outdoors have always played a big role in shaping her creative process.

Natalie earned her bachelor of arts from UC Santa Cruz and her master of fine arts from the Massachusetts College of Art and Design. Her work has been shown both nationally and internationally, at venues including Benrubi Gallery in New York and the Santa Cruz Museum of Art and History. In 2024, she was the Post Graduate Teaching Fellow at the Massachusetts College of Art and Design. She currently lives and works in California.

Natalie enjoys the collaborative nature of portraiture, where the photographer and the subject work together to tell a story through a single frame. For Natalie, it's all about building a connection with the person she's photographing, making them feel comfortable so that their true selves come through in the image. She's drawn to capturing the unique qualities of each individual and finds it incredibly rewarding to create images that feel both personal and meaningful to them.

Dr. Donna Rena Walton, EdD

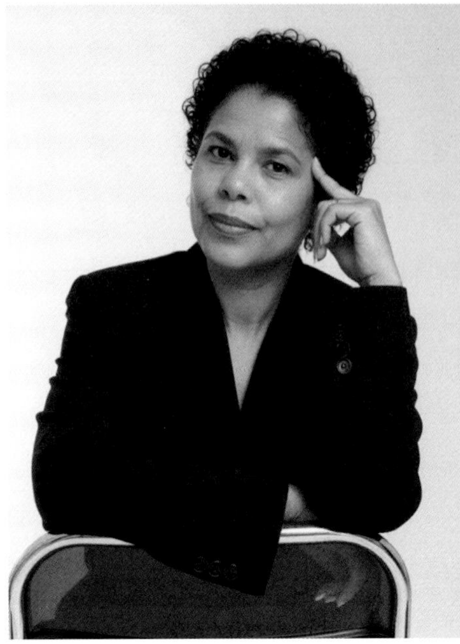

Dr. Donna R. Walton, EdD is a nationally recognized disability advocate, strategist, speaker, actress, and author whose career spans over three decades across higher education, public service, private industry, and nonprofit leadership. She is the Founder and President of the Divas With Disabilities Project, a nonprofit organization that elevates the voices and visibility of disabled women of color through media, mentorship, and visibility centered activism.

Dr. Walton began her professional journey in academia, teaching undergraduate and graduate level courses in education and rehabilitation counseling. Her work in higher education laid the foundation for a lifelong commitment to equity, empowerment, and inclusive leadership. She later transitioned into federal service, where she led initiatives focused on disability employment, workforce development, and civil rights compliance. Her contributions in both public and private sectors have shaped inclusive hiring practices, advanced policy implementation, and bridged gaps between compliance and community impact.

An accomplished author, Dr. Walton penned Shattered Dreams, Broken Pieces, a powerful memoir chronicling her journey through loss, resilience, and radical self acceptance. Her writing, like her advocacy, challenges perceptions and invites readers to reimagine disability as a source of strength and creativity.

Dr. Walton is also a seasoned actress whose credits include the Hulu series The Other Black Girl, the digital series The Retreat, and numerous national commercials. Her performances reflect her commitment to authentic representation and her belief that visibility is a form of advocacy. Whether on screen or on stage, she brings depth, dignity, and charisma to every role.

As a sought after motivational speaker, Dr. Walton has delivered keynote addresses, workshops, and trainings nationwide—sharing her lived experience as a Black woman, above the knee amputee, and cancer survivor to inspire transformation and action. Her message is clear: disability is not a deficit, but a dimension of leadership, artistry, and legacy.

Dr. Walton holds advanced degrees in education and rehabilitation counseling, and her impact has been recognized by numerous organizations committed to equity and disability justice. Whether mentoring emerging leaders, advancing disability equity, commanding the stage as a performer and speaker, or curating gatherings that foster inclusion, access, and shared empowerment, she leads with clarity, compassion, and conviction.

About the Author

Jennifer Chassman Browne

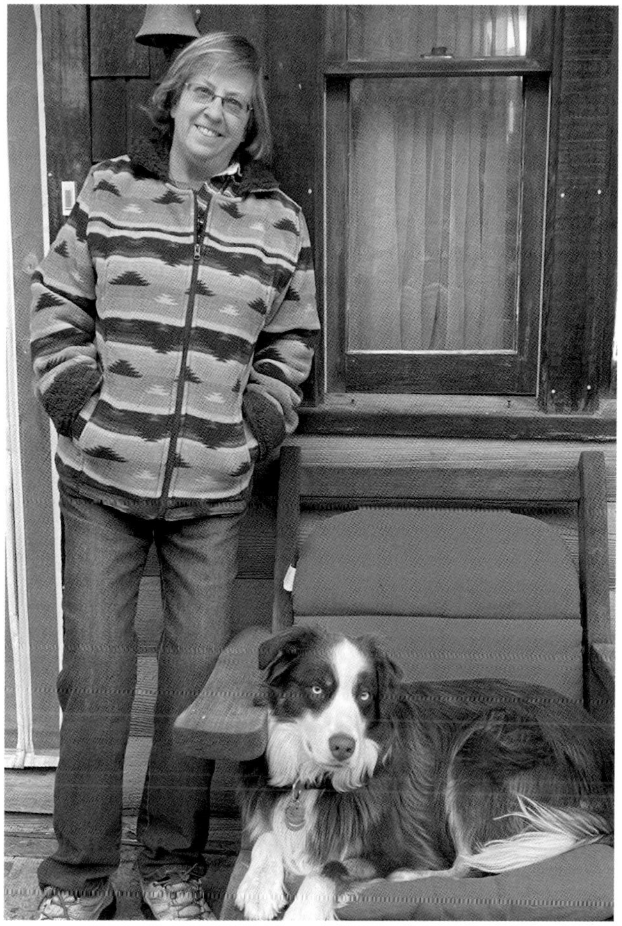

Jenn has lived with rheumatoid arthritis since she was six years old. While she was an active and athletic child, as an adult, her arthritis has become more limiting.

It's been a challenging process for her to redefine her sense of self and to accept these limitations while still trying to move forward and to work around them. Despite her disability, she has been able to remain active.

For most of her professional life, Jenn has been an English teacher and school leader and has loved the time that she spent with the teenagers that she taught, many of whom she still has in her life.

For the past seven years, she has worked as a DEI and disability advocate.

In her work as a disability advocate and educator, she brings disability awareness into all of the work that she does. Too often, serving people with disabilities is not part of the national conversation. She helps the people with whom she works to consider how we can create a world that is more inclusive of all people, including people with disabilities.

Jenn works to educate people about the strengths and gifts that people with disabilities have. Everyone has something that limits them, and success asks that we simply move forward even with the limitations that we have. That said, we need allies, systems, and structures that ensure our inclusion and success.

Jenn has also earned certification as a listener poet and is invested in working with organizations to use the listener poet process as part of a support system for those in careers with a high emotional demand.

Jenn loves writing and collaborated with her husband, Kevin, on a poetry collection last year. She most enjoys spending time with her sweetie and her pup, Indy, at home on the central coast of California.

Fists Clenched

It wasn't until
I looked down
And saw my own hands,
Clenched into fists
Of defense
And defiance
That I realized how I was carrying myself.
And how much I was carrying
Each day.

Having to steel myself
Against the world
Of judgments
Of unforgiving stares
That see only my awkward gait and knobby hands
The avalanche of glances, comments, and actions grow
Until I am buried in
"Can I help you with that...let me do that for you...what's wrong with you...you're almost there and doing great..."
Worse even when the chair that I'm sitting in is pulled, almost out from under me.
The package I'm carrying yanked from my hands,
My slowly-bending leg grabbed and bent by the person behind me boarding the bus.
Never asked -
I've become an object to be moved without permission.
An obstacle, hindering others' progress.

Helpers, they call themselves,
Doing a kindness for the poor disabled girl.
They must feel good about providing assistance.
Their altruism, a badge of pride.

But I am not your inspiration
Oh, no,
I'm your worst nightmare
To wake up in a body like mine...
Broken and scarred
From the inside out.
Betraying me with each step.
The idea so terrifying,
While perhaps inevitable,
It must be avoided.

And thus, in your insistence to help
You've created distance-
Keeping me at an "I-am-not-like-you" arm's length
Must allow you to breathe more easily.
Making it clear that the problem is mine,
That you are the savior,
The giver of aid.
The able-bodied.
Acting based on the assumption
That I am incapable
Of caring for myself.
Making the judgment
That because I do things differently
I must be in need of help.

Perhaps it is agonizing for you to watch me;
My perceived suffering
Causing you pain
That you want to mitigate, alleviate.
And so you offer assistance,
Insistently so,
Even when I say, "no"
You question my ability to know
For myself,
What I need or don't need.
Forcing me to be only what my body appears.
Though I am much more,
I'm made so small
By your estimation
Of my limited capacity.

It's so hard for me to hold my tongue-
For when I don't
It's forked and venomous-
I spit rage.
Rage that further widens the chasm
Between able and disabled.
Becoming an angry
Handicapped woman
Who can be dismissed-
My behavior explained away
As self-loathing;
A lack of self-esteem.
Either way, it's about me.
I am the one with the problem,
And if I respond as I'd like,
I am the one with the bad attitude as well.

And so I keep my comments to myself,
Not wanting to become what you already believe me to be.

But there is a cost in holding my tongue-
The venom seeps
Into my own body-
Growing within rather than escaping.
I remain trapped by it,
It poisons my thoughts and feelings about myself,
Until I can only see me through the eyes of others.
Saddened by what I see-
Hurt and angry.

And so I know that I must express myself,
Must find a way
To make you really see me,
The me that is more than
A hand or a knee.
To see
Beyond this body,
This imperfect shell.
To the whole person
Who is strong, independent, and capable
And who wants to see herself as such.

And as I know no other way,
I'll use my voice,
Soft or loud,
Kind or angry.
No longer invisible,
Though still carrying this weight,
I speak
So that I can finally
Unclench my fists.

—Jennifer Chassman Browne